LEADING THE WAY THROUGH
DANIEL

MICHAEL YOUSSEF

HARVEST HOUSE PUBLISHERS
EUGENE, OREGON

LEADING THE WAY THROUGH DANIEL
Copyright © 2012 by Michael Youssef
Published by Harvest House Publishers
Eugene, Oregon 97402
www.harvesthousepublishers.com

Library of Congress Cataloging-in-Publication Data

Youssef, Michael.
    Leading the way through Daniel/Michael Youssef.
        p.cm.
    ISBN 978-0-7369-5164-7 (pbk.)
    ISBN 978-0-7369-5165-4 (eBook)
    1. Bible. O.T. Daniel—Criticism, interpretation, etc. 2. Daniel (Biblical figure) I. Title.
    BS1555.52.Y68 2012
    224'.507—dc23

                                                    2012020304

Printed in the United States of America

                12 13 14 15 16 17 18 19 20 / VP-NI / 10 9 8 7 6 5 4 3 2 1

To all faithful preachers, teachers, and Christian leaders
who seek to accurately expound the Word of God
from pulpits or in Sunday school classes or in home Bible study groups.

Acknowledgments

First, I offer all my thanksgiving to the Father in heaven whose Holy Spirit has laid on my heart the writing of this series for the glory of Jesus. I am also immensely grateful to the Lord for sending me an able and gifted editor and compiler of my material in Jim Denney.

Special thanks to the entire team at Harvest House Publishers—and especially to Bob Hawkins Jr., LaRae Weikert, and Rod Morris, who shared my vision and made this dream a reality.

My expression of thanks would not be complete without mentioning the patience and perseverance of Robert and Andrew Wolgemuth of Wolgemuth and Associates, Inc. literary agency for managing the many details of such an undertaking.

My earnest prayer is that, as I leave this legacy to the next generation, God would raise up great men and women to faithfully serve their generation by accurately interpreting the Word of God.

Contents

Introduction

Can One Person Make a Difference?

In March 2005, I returned from an international speaking trip to find my home city, Atlanta, in the grip of terror. On Friday, March 11, a man named Brian Nichols was transported to the new Justice Tower in downtown Atlanta for his retrial on rape and other violent felony charges. As a woman deputy removed Nichols's handcuffs to allow him to change into civilian clothes, he brutally beat her, stole her gun, and escaped.

In a daylong rampage, Nichols shot five people, hijacked cars, and melted into the crowd at Lenox Square in Buckhead, not far from our church. No one knew where he had gone—or where he might appear next. One person, one evildoer, had thrown a major metroplex into panic.

A couple of hours after midnight, another person entered the story—a woman named Ashley Smith. This young woman had recently committed her life to Christ and was seeking to grow in a relationship with the Lord. Her husband had been murdered several years before, and she was looking for a new job to better provide for herself and her five-year-old daughter. She had just moved to a new apartment and was unpacking boxes at 2:00 a.m. when she decided to run a quick errand to a convenience store. It was a fateful decision.

As she left her apartment, Ashley noticed a man sitting in a pickup nearby. He was still there when she returned a few minutes later. As she inserted her key in the front door, the man came up behind her and forced her into the apartment. Ashley realized she had just been taken hostage by Brian Nichols.

The fugitive gunman tied Ashley up with an extension cord, then sat down and began talking with her. She explained to Nichols that her husband had been murdered, and if he killed her as well, her little girl would be left with no mommy and no daddy. The nightmare of Ashley's captivity continued through the night, and she kept talking to Nichols, trying to gain his trust. She asked if she could read to him, and he agreed. So Ashley read aloud from her Bible and from a devotional book.

Nichols told her he had hurt some people, and he didn't want to hurt anyone else. He just wanted to rest in her home for a few days. As Ashley continued talking to Nichols about her family and her faith, he told her that he was lost and he believed God led him to her. He even called her an "angel" sent from God.

"What do you think I should do?" he asked.

"Turn yourself in," she said. "If you don't, lots more people are going to get hurt. And you're probably going to die."

As he watched news reports about his escape and crime spree on TV, he said, "I cannot believe that's me."

Finally, Nichols let Ashley go. She left the apartment and immediately called 911. Moments later, at ten in the morning, a SWAT team arrived at the apartment. By noon, police had taken Nichols into custody without incident.

Ashley Smith was praised for her courage and levelheaded thinking during the hours she was held hostage. She was interviewed many times on television, and witnessed to her faith in Jesus Christ before millions of TV viewers nationwide. Her witness to Brian Nichols spared her life, and probably spared his life as well. Her witness also blessed the nation.

She told the press, "I have experienced just about every emotion one can imagine in the span of just a few days. Throughout my time with Mr. Nichols, I continued to rely on my faith in God. God has helped me through tough times before, and he'll help me now… Thank you for your prayers and may God bless you all."[1]

Can one person make a difference? Absolutely! One person can make a difference for evil—or for good. That difference may impact one life or it may impact millions of lives. The difference one life makes could have eternal consequences. That's the overarching theme of the book of Daniel: One committed believer can make all the difference in the world.

Now, more than ever before, we need to understand the lessons of the life of Daniel—lessons in making a world-changing difference for God. One person plus God is always a majority. No matter how troubled the world may be, no matter how dark and terrifying the circumstances, you can be God's chosen instrument making a positive difference at the crossroads of history.

That was the theme of Daniel's life. And it can be the theme of your life as well. Turn the page with me as we plunge into Bible history, and together let's discover God's amazing plan for your future.

1

Your Indelible Identity

Daniel 1:1-9

O nce, while visiting a friend, I was in his kitchen and saw a little postcard taped to the refrigerator door. It read: "Remember, God has something up his sleeve besides his everlasting arm."

That is good advice, and we should remember those words whenever we are under pressure, under threat, or under stress. No matter how bleak our situation, God always has something up his sleeve. He always has a plan and a purpose for our lives—and for the ages. His plan covers every detail, every need, every problem of your life.

Now, that doesn't mean that you and I will necessarily understand his plan in our lifetime. We could not begin to comprehend his Master Blueprint for the universe or for our individual lives. Our minds are finite and his is infinite. For reasons that are often baffling to us, God sometimes allows us to go through intense pressure and trouble. We all experience good times and bad times in varying proportions. No one understood this principle better than this faithful prophet of the Old Testament.

In the third year of the reign of King Jehoiakim, 605 BC, the Babylonian army rumbled like a juggernaut across the land of Israel, destroying Jerusalem and laying waste the villages and the country-side. Daniel and his people were captured and led away in chains into captivity in Babylon. There Daniel was educated in the philosophies and pagan ideas of Babylon.

Though Daniel was taught these alien and ungodly ways, he never embraced them or converted to them. He remained true to the God of Israel in his heart. Because Daniel embraced the true wisdom of his God, his reputation grew and he became a prominent advisor in the royal court of Babylon. He was one of the bright, rising stars of Israel who served in the court of King Nebuchadnezzar of Babylon. There, he experienced the fullness of God's purpose for his life.

Even though Daniel experienced suffering, anxiety, humiliation, and persecution as a captive of the Babylonians, God had a plan for Daniel's life. It was not a backup plan. God did not have to shift from Plan A to Plan B because of unexpected circumstances. The Babylonian invasion did not come as a surprise to God. All the events of Daniel's life were accounted for by God, and he worked all of those events together in Daniel's life to accomplish his positive purpose in a negative world. God had a plan to use Daniel as a strong witness for his truth and a strong encouragement for his people, even though they were exiles in a heathen land.

A limitless God

Here is the beginning of Daniel's story:

> In the third year of the reign of Jehoiakim king of Judah, Nebuchadnezzar king of Babylon came to Jerusalem and besieged it. And the Lord gave Jehoiakim king of Judah into his hand, with some of the vessels of the house of God. And he brought them to the land of Shinar, to the

house of his god, and placed the vessels in the treasury of his god. Then the king commanded Ashpenaz, his chief eunuch, to bring some of the people of Israel, both of the royal family and of the nobility, youths without blemish, of good appearance and skillful in all wisdom, endowed with knowledge, understanding learning, and competent to stand in the king's palace, and to teach them the literature and language of the Chaldeans. The king assigned them a daily portion of the food that the king ate, and of the wine that he drank. They were to be educated for three years, and at the end of that time they were to stand before the king. Among these were Daniel, Hananiah, Mishael, and Azariah of the tribe of Judah. And the chief of the eunuchs gave them names: Daniel he called Belteshazzar, Hananiah he called Shadrach, Mishael he called Meshach, and Azariah he called Abednego (Daniel 1:1-7).

God provided for Daniel in exile. He placed Daniel in the king's most elite training and education program. He arranged for a mentoring relationship between Daniel and one of the king's most trusted aides. And Daniel remained faithful to the God of Israel. So, in verse 9, we see that God gave Daniel favor and compassion in the sight of the chief of the eunuchs. God elevated Daniel to a position of far-reaching impact and influence. Not only did Daniel's influence affect the king, and through the king the entire kingdom of Babylon, but his influence has echoed down through the ages, affecting millions of believers, including you and me.

Daniel is a role model, an example to us of the power of one person to make a difference. His story speaks to us across the ages and reminds us of what God is able to do through the life of one yielded, faithful servant. As we witness the life of this committed young man, let's open our minds and hearts to believe that God can do anything—*absolutely anything!*—through our lives as well.

One of the key lessons of Daniel's life is that God is with us in times of trial, persecution, and temptation. We can always count on God to have a plan and a purpose for the difficult circumstances we face. His purposes are ultimately for *eternal good*.

God's power is never wasted. God's plan is never thwarted. Everything he does is focused on a purpose—and his purposes are not bound to any finite time or fixed place. God's purposes are for eternity. No matter what happens to you, if you will stand firm on God's principles as Daniel did, if you will trust God to work in you and through you and around you as Daniel did, you can have 100 percent confidence that what God has planned for your life will have an *eternal* impact.

This is great news! It means that when you and God lock arms—your finite, earthly arms linked with his infinite, everlasting arms—you cannot fail. You *will* have an impact on your world. You *will* have an impact on eternity. Every act of kindness you perform, every word of blessing you speak, every stand you take for truth and righteousness, and every godly relationship you maintain becomes a building block God uses to construct his kingdom.

In this life, you may experience what looks like a setback, a failure, the end of everything—but God has something up his sleeve. You may be surprised by the events of this life, but nothing surprises him. So take heart. You are never alone. Your faithfulness and willingness to stand against pressure and persecution will not go unnoticed. You are connected to a limitless God. The power he makes available to you is as unlimited as God himself.

Who are you?

What is your nickname? If you're a doctor or a professor, people may call you Doc. If you work with electrical equipment, people may call you Sparky. If you have a reputation for being especially brainy, then you've probably been called Einstein a time or two. A tall and slender physique will earn you the nickname Slim or Beanpole. I once heard of one man who nicknamed his wife Red when they were in their twenties and her hair was auburn, and he continued to call her Red long after her hair had turned completely gray.

Often, it's your surname that gives you away. When my Atlanta neighbors hear my last name, Youssef, they instantly know that I'm not from around these parts, even though I have lived in Atlanta for more than three decades. They don't have to see my face or hear my voice; they just have to hear my name to know that I'm not a good ol' boy from the South.

In the ancient world, your name was your identity. Your name didn't merely mark you as a member of this family or that clan. Your name said something about you. It described the kind of person you were. It especially described your character.

Most babies in Bible times were not named until eight days after their birth. This gave parents a little time to notice the characteristics of their child—not just physical traits but personality traits, behavior, and other indications about that child's true nature. It was a custom in Bible times for mothers to spend hours singing and talking to their newborn children, bonding with them in a deeply emotional and spiritual way. Through this time of bonding, mothers could gain a special insight into the personalities and even the destinies of their children.

The book of Daniel tells the story of four young men of Israel— Daniel and his three companions. Each of these young men had a name that revealed much about his character. When they were born, their parents gave them names that *revealed* their identity and character and helped *shape* their identity and character.

- Daniel's name meant "God has judged."
- Hananiah's name meant "Yahweh has been gracious."
- Mishael's name meant "Who is like God?"
- Azariah's name meant "Yahweh has helped."

Each of these names is fitting in its own way. Daniel's name is especially appropriate because the prophet Daniel repeatedly prophesied God's judgment upon the idolatry and arrogance of the Gentile nation of Babylon. Moreover, the book of Daniel makes clear that he was gifted in administration, and he exercised wise and godly judgment throughout his career.

Hananiah's name was equally fitting. He knew the gracious nature of God. Mishael understood that there was nobody else like God. Azariah knew that Yahweh was still the One who helped them. These three men knew without any doubt that God's mercy and sovereign protection were behind the miracles they experienced throughout their years in Babylon.

These four young men were just teenagers when the Babylonian invaders tore them away from their families and their homeland. Daniel was only fourteen years old, and he was probably the oldest of the four.

God allowed King Nebuchadnezzar to conquer the land of Israel and take some of the best and brightest of Israel's youth, along with the wealth of the nation. God told Israel through his prophets that Israel's captivity would last seventy years, but Daniel and his friends didn't know with certainty that they would live to see Israel's captivity end. As far as they knew, they would live out their lives and die in Babylon.

Nebuchadnezzar was ruthless—and smart. He prized talent, intelligence, and ability, and these four young men of Israel possessed all of these qualities. So Nebuchadnezzar took the cream of Israel's male population to the city of Babylon and subjected them to a training regimen so intense it bordered on brainwashing. Nebuchadnezzar planned to use these brilliant young men as tools to expand his power and influence in the world, but first he had to bend them to his purposes.

The first step in indoctrinating these young men was to give them new Babylonian identities that would cancel out their Jewish identity as servants of the God of Israel. According to their new Babylonian names, they were now the servants of pagan Babylonian deities. The chief of the eunuchs gave Daniel the Babylonian name Belteshazzar, which means "keeper of the hidden treasure of Bel." Bel was the supreme Babylonian deity. In fact, Bel was another name for Baal, a false god who was well-known to the Israelites because Baal was worshipped by their enemies in Canaan.

Hananiah was renamed Shadrach, a name linked to the Babylonian moon god. Mishael was renamed Meshach, corrupting the meaning of his name from "Who is like God?" to "Who is like the moon god?" And Azariah was renamed Abednego, meaning he was a servant of the Babylonian god of wisdom, Nego (or Nabu). Nebuchadnezzar had uprooted their identity. No longer were these young men to be known as servants of the God of Israel. Henceforth, they were to be called servants of the gods of Babylon.

Even though the Babylonians changed their names, these courageous and faithful Hebrew teenagers refused to let go of their identity as servants of Yahweh. They continued to worship their God. They continued to pray to him and trust him. Everything about their speech and behavior reflected their belief in Yahweh and their utter rejection of the pagan gods of Babylon. This is a crucial lesson for you and me today.

Who does God say you are?

The Babylonians tried to alter the identity of these four young Hebrew men by changing their names, but the attempt failed. It didn't matter what the Babylonians called Daniel, Hananiah, Mishael, and Azariah. God still knew them by their original names—names that spoke of his ownership of their lives. God still knew them as God-Has-Judged, Yahweh-Has-Been-Gracious, Who-Is-Like-God? and Yahweh-Has-Helped.

And God loves and knows you in exactly the same way. The world may try to slap another label on you. Some people might call you Religious Fanatic, Goody Two-shoes, Bible Thumper, or Pulpit Pounder. Some perfectly decent Christians have been labeled Intolerant Extremists or American Taliban because they dared to suggest that godliness and moral values produce a happier and healthier society. But no matter what label the world tries to impose on you, God knows you by the beautiful label of *Christian.* You wear the name of his Son, Jesus Christ. Because you follow Jesus, because you accept the shed blood of Christ as the atonement for your sins, the name of Jesus is written on your life. When God calls you his beloved child, that is your true identity.

God has a unique plan and purpose for your life. Nobody else can fulfill your part of God's plan—only *you.* As you embrace the truth that you are a unique and irreplaceable part of God's plan, then you begin to understand what the power of one really means. You were not created to be like any other person. Your role is to be the one and only irreplaceable you that God created you to be.

Do you truly believe that you are the person God says you are? Do you trust him to carry out his eternal plan through your life? Do you believe he is willing and able to use you to accomplish great things for his kingdom? God's Word tells us that, as people who have received Jesus Christ as Lord and Savior, we are:

- *Righteous.* We have "right standing" with God. We are not righteous because of what *we* have accomplished or earned, but because of what *Jesus* accomplished for us on the cross. (See Romans 3:21-22; 5:19; 10:4.)

- *Forgiven.* The slate of your past and mine has been wiped clean. Now we are free to move forward with our lives— and free to serve God and receive his blessings and rewards. (See Ephesians 1:7; Colossians 1:13-14; 1 John 1:9; 2:12.)

- *Destined for eternal life.* Our heavenly home is already under construction because of what Jesus has done on our behalf. (See John 3:16; 3:36; 6:40; 17:3; Romans 6:23; 1 Timothy 1:16; Titus 3:4-7; 1 John 5:11.)

- *Indwelt by the Holy Spirit.* The Spirit of Truth is present in the lives of all who have received Jesus as Lord and Savior. He leads us and guides us into the right way to respond in all situations. The Holy Spirit gives us the power to obey God's commandments and to live changed lives. (See John 7:37-39; 1 Corinthians 6:19-20; Ephesians 1:13.)

- *Beloved of God.* The Bible gives us a long list of attributes that God has for his children. Perhaps the most important of those attributes is that we are *beloved*. We are God's cherished children, heirs with Jesus Christ of the fullness of God's kingdom. (See John 14:21; Romans 1:7; 1 Thessalonians 1:4; 2 Thessalonians 2:16.)

If you don't know what God says about you, if you don't know that his name is stamped upon you, then you will continually find yourself intimidated and swayed by the labels others put on you. The world will call you Wimp for turning the other cheek when people persecute you—but God will commend you for your Christ-like strength. The world will call you Stupid for giving sacrificially to the work of God—but God will bring you a harvest of blessings. The world will call you Weak because you need religion as your spiritual crutch—but God will make his infinite power available to you in a way that will astound the world.

Don't trust the world to give you your identity. The identity the world gives you is flawed and false. As the apostle Paul writes, "Do not be conformed to this world, but be transformed by the renewal of your mind, that by testing you may discern what is the will of God, what is good and acceptable and perfect" (Romans

12:2). Don't chase after the identities that are prized in this world: Rich, Successful, Powerful, Famous, or Cool. There's nothing necessarily wrong with having money, success, authority, fame—and there's not even anything wrong with being cool. But don't chase after those things. Seek first the kingdom of God and his righteousness, as Jesus said, and God will provide everything you need (see Matthew 6:33).

It is God who elevates some to positions of prominence. It is God who gives people the ability and opportunity to make money and manage it well. It is God who allows us to live, who keeps our hearts beating and our lungs breathing, so that we can live and work each day. It is God who gives each of us the ability to forgive, to love, to experience joy, and to be patient in difficult times.

Accomplishments are fleeting. Opinions are subject to change. The world's definitions are constantly being revised. But God's definitions do not change because God does not change. What he says about us has eternity written all over it. God says that if you believe in his Son, his name is indelibly stamped on your life—and nothing in this world can ever change that.

Jesus gave us his name

When Jesus gave us his name, he gave us his identity. The word *Christian* literally means "little Christ" or "one who is like Christ." The word *Christian* refers to a person so Christlike that people think they are seeing Jesus himself. As Christians, our words and actions should mirror those of the Lord. Our way of life should embody what Jesus would do if he were walking in our world today.

Your supreme identity is all bound up in the word *Christian*. The world may know me as Michael, and it may know you as Jim or Joe or Jane or Jill, but that is not your true identity. You are a Christian. You bear the name of Christ. You represent Christ to the world. Above all else, that is who you truly are.

Jesus once told his followers, "If you ask me anything in my name, I will do it" (John 14:14). He gave his followers the authority to heal the sick and cast out demons in his name. He gave them the ability to solve problems and meet human needs in his name. Because Jesus has given us his name and his full identity, we have the power and authority to stand confidently in the midst of a fallen and sinful world and say, "I choose this day whom I will serve, and I choose to serve Jesus."

As you go out into the world today—to your place of employment, your neighborhood, your place of ministry—you can say to yourself, "I am going out into the world in the name of Jesus. Everything I do, I do in the identity of Jesus. It is as if Jesus himself were wearing these clothes, walking in these shoes. I wear his name, and everything I do, I do in the name of Jesus."

Then, everywhere you go throughout your day, walk in the identity of Jesus. Do what he would do, say what he would say. Be Jesus to everyone around you. You may be all they ever see or know of Jesus in the course of this day, so wear his name well.

The pagan world tried to change the names of Daniel, Hananiah, Mishael, and Azariah to names that reflected the false gods of Babylon. But the pagan world could not change the true identities of these four heroic young men of Israel. God's name was written in their hearts and on their lives. So God gave Daniel and his companions favor and success, even in the land of their captivity.

2

Challenging the
Status Quo

Daniel 1:1-2,5-9

I was born in Egypt. When I was twenty years old, I moved from the Middle East to Australia. No world could have been more foreign to me. My accent gave me away at every turn. My familiarity with the English language was nowhere near what it is today. I continually ran afoul of customs and cultural norms without realizing what I was doing wrong. I felt adrift—and I could identify with Moses who said during his exile in the Egyptian wilderness that he felt like "a stranger in a strange land" (Exodus 2:22 KJV).

Had I not been in the company of Christians who believed in the same God I worshipped and knew the same Bible that I read, I would have felt overwhelmed. I spent many hours watching and listening to the people around me in order to learn how to fit in to this new culture I was suddenly immersed in. I knew I'd be studying in Australia for several years, so I needed to come to grips with the culture.

Daniel and his friends probably understood that feeling very well. They too were strangers in a strange land. They had a good idea just how far they were from their homeland. They had made the trek from Jerusalem to Babylon on foot and in chains. They had experienced language shock and culture shock. They had experienced the cruelty of a pitiless conqueror. Babylon could never truly be home to these four young men. It would always be a land of exile, a strange land.

There is an important lesson for you and me in the exile experience of Daniel, Hananiah, Mishael, and Azariah. It's important to remember that the land we live in is not our home. In fact, this entire planet is not our home. It's not our eternal destiny. The Bible clearly tells us that heaven is our home and we are just passing through this wilderness called earth. As the apostle Peter writes, "conduct yourselves with fear throughout the time of your exile" (1 Peter 1:17).

We also need to understand that we live in a post-Christian age. Western civilization, which was largely the product of Christian culture and tradition, is crumbling. And even though many Christians are living in America today, we have to acknowledge that the United States of America, which was founded on Christian principles, no longer lives up to those principles.

Exiles in post-Christian America

The founding fathers of the United States were, for the most part, Christians. The principles embedded in the Constitution and other founding documents gave the nation and its government a largely Christian tone and character. Concepts such as liberty, equality, justice, fairness, and tolerance for individual differences come straight from the Christian Scriptures. These concepts helped shape our national character for two hundred years. The state constitution of every one of the thirteen original states made reference to divine destiny and reliance upon God.

This is not to say that America was ever a theocracy or that Christianity was the official state religion of the United States. Religious freedom and pluralism have always been essential principles of our government. But our founding fathers acknowledged that America could not expect to remain free without a foundation of faith in God.

John Adams expressed it this way: "It is religion and morality alone which can establish the principles upon which freedom can securely stand." And Benjamin Franklin said, "The longer I live, the more convincing proofs I see of this truth, that God governs in the affairs of men. And if a sparrow cannot fall to the ground without His notice, is it probable that an empire can rise without His aid? We have been assured, Sir, in the Sacred Writings, that 'except the Lord build the House, they labor in vain that build it.'"

So while America has never had a state church or state religion and has never been a theocracy, neither has America ever been a purely secular state that rejected the role of faith in public life.

Until now.

America today is truly no longer a Christian nation. The majority of people in America do not live devout Christian lives. They may call themselves Christians, but they don't exemplify the teachings of the Christian Scriptures. They don't demand Christian behavior and Christian integrity from their leaders. They don't demand that the laws of the land be informed by biblical principles of truth and justice. They don't live out Christian integrity in the workplace, nor insist that values, virtue, morality, and respect for God be taught in the public schools.

In post-Christian America, several hundred thousand unborn babies are killed every year for the sake of convenience. We value the lives of endangered whales, endangered birds, and even stray cats and dogs more than we value the lives of unborn human beings.

Here in post-Christian America, our entertainment media applaud every sexual perversion imaginable, yet nightly mock and ridicule Christians and even Christ himself. Just a few years ago, it would have been inconceivable that any television network, let alone one owned by the Walt Disney Company, would air a television show such as the one called *GCB*. Those letters stand for *Good Christian…* and a word I will not put in print. This "comedy," which I'm glad to report was recently cancelled by ABC, depicted Christians in a Dallas suburb engaging in adultery, homosexuality, pornography, and self-righteous hypocritical judgment toward one another. While it's true that hypocrisy and sin exist in the church, the message of the show was that hypocrisy and sin are pretty much *all there is* to being a Christian.

Today in post-Christian America, there is only one activity that secularists are willing to label a sin, and that is the sin of intolerance. It is a virtue to tolerate all forms of sin, say the secularists, and it's a "sin" to hate sin. To the secularists, it's a sin to say that sin is wrong. It's a sin to say that sex is only for marriage, that marriage should be defined as one man and one woman, that abortion is wrong, or that fatherless homes are not the best environment in which to raise children. To say such things, according to the secularists, is intolerant "hate speech."

Yet it is apparently not a sin, according to the secularists, to be intolerant of Christianity. It is perfectly okay to defame and slander Christians, Christianity, and Christ himself in the media. The producers of a television show like *GCB* actually hoped that Christians would protest and boycott the show, because controversy means publicity, ratings, and higher profits. So Christians in post-Christian America are in a lose-lose situation. America was once a Christian nation, but not anymore.

Like Daniel, Hananiah, Mishael, and Azariah, you and I are strangers in a strange land. Post-Christian America is not our home. If you were born in America, if you are a true and faithful worshipper of Christ, then you are an exile in the land of your birth.

Why was Israel held captive?

Why were Daniel and his friends exiled to Babylon? Why did God allow Israel to be held captive by a pagan nation?

The nation of Israel had turned a deaf ear to the Word of God and had rejected the warnings of the prophet Jeremiah. God's patience with his people had run out. So he allowed King Nebuchadnezzar, emperor of the Babylonian Empire, to invade Israel, lay siege to Jerusalem, ravage the nation, and enslave its people. The Bible tells us:

> In the third year of the reign of Jehoiakim king of Judah, Nebuchadnezzar king of Babylon came to Jerusalem and besieged it. And the Lord gave Jehoiakim king of Judah into his hand, with some of the vessels of the house of God. And he brought them to the land of Shinar, to the house of his god, and placed the vessels in the treasury of his god (1:1-2).

How could God do this? We like to think of God in terms of his love and mercy—and without question, the God of the Bible is a God of mercy. But he's also a God of justice. And we need to recognize the balance between God's mercy and God's justice. God will not tolerate ongoing rebellion. He places a limit on our willful disobedience to his commandments. He will even allow enemies to strike at us and sometimes take us captive, not because he hates us, but in order to chasten us and bring us to our senses so that we will return to him.

God chastises us in order to warn us and help us to realize the danger we are in. Our disobedience toward God imperils us on every level—physical, moral, psychological, and spiritual. Sinful disobedience toward God can produce physical illness, poverty, broken relationships, scandal and disgrace, mental and emotional deterioration, and even death—both physical and spiritual death. God in his love wants to spare us from the self-destruction of our own sin. If we are living in a right relationship with him, he does not need to chasten us. But if we are living in open rebellion toward him, his chastening is often the only way he can get our attention.

So discover what God wants to teach you. Learn the lessons he has for you, especially the lessons of obedience and humility. If you find that your enemies are striking at you, if you feel you have been taken captive in some area of your life, ask God to show you what you should do in order to return to a right relationship with him.

Learn from the disobedience of Israel.

A refusal to compromise

Learn also from the obedience and wisdom of Daniel and his friends. Even though their nation was being chastised for its rebellion against God, these four young men were role models of godliness and a righteous way of life.

> The king assigned them a daily portion of the food that the king ate, and of the wine that he drank. They were to be educated for three years, and at the end of that time they were to stand before the king. Among these were Daniel, Hananiah, Mishael, and Azariah of the tribe of Judah. And the chief of the eunuchs gave them names: Daniel he called Belteshazzar, Hananiah he called Shadrach, Mishael he called Meshach, and Azariah he called Abednego.
>
> But Daniel resolved that he would not defile himself with the king's food, or with the wine that he drank. Therefore he asked the chief of the eunuchs to allow him not to defile himself. And God gave Daniel favor and compassion in the sight of the chief of the eunuchs (1:5-9).

Daniel and his friends were exceptionally bright young men who had been ripped away from their families by force. They had left behind everything they knew—their culture, language, temple, family, and friends—and they were forced to march hundreds of miles across the wilderness to a place of strange customs, a strange language, and above all, a strange religion and belief system. They were shocked, confused, and overwhelmed by all of these new experiences—and by everything they had lost.

At the same time, we should acknowledge that culture shock can sometimes be a good thing. It can help us see our cultural assumptions from a new perspective. A young woman recently told me, "I tried to imagine my great-grandmother sitting next to me on the sofa watching television last night. I could almost feel the embarrassment she would have felt watching all those sexually suggestive commercials, let alone the immorality of the shows themselves. A lot of the raunchy humor probably would have gone right over her head, but what she could understand would have offended her. It saddened me to realize that the things that shocked my great-grandmother don't even faze me. I'm so used to watching filth on TV that I'm not even repulsed anymore—and that's not good!"

She's right. It's not good to lose our ability to be shocked and offended by the moral sewage that surrounds us. If we are no longer shocked and offended by blasphemy and obscenity, then we have ceased to be at war with this fallen world. We have surrendered to its influence.

Daniel and his friends were acutely aware of the nightmarish conditions in which they lived. They had been torn away from their homeland and sent to an alien land that worshipped pagan demon-gods. The stark contrast between God's ways and the ways of Babylon undoubtedly contributed to the moral and spiritual clarity these young men displayed.

What made their ordeal all the more enticing and seductive was that they were not, strictly speaking, imprisoned or enslaved. Rather, they were placed in luxurious surroundings in Babylon. They lived in the palace of King Nebuchadnezzar, and they were surrounded by pleasures and enticements. Even though they had been forced into exile under violent circumstances, they landed in the lap of luxury. No doubt, these young men felt a certain degree of curiosity and wonder at everything they saw—the beautiful buildings and gardens of Babylon, and the furnishings of gold, silver, and fine imported fabrics. All the luxuries of the ancient world were placed at their disposal.

So Daniel and his companions faced a dilemma, and it is much like the dilemma you and I face. We live in a world that is hostile to our faith, our values, and our beliefs, yet it also offers many materialistic enticements and sensuous delights. We are tempted to wonder, *Can such a world of luxury and wealth be so bad? Can the things of this world be so wrong if they feel so right?*

But Daniel and his friends possessed a wisdom that you and I would do well to emulate. They concluded that the pleasure and opulence of the world are a mere façade. At its core, the world of Babylon, like our world, is not merely indifferent to Jesus Christ; it is actively hostile. Although the world demands tolerance from Christians, it will not tolerate genuine Christians. Instead, our post-Christian world insists that we accept their godless belief system, their corrosive values, and their hedonistic lifestyles. The world continually pressures us as Christians to become *less* Christlike, less pure, less faithful, less moral. Tragically, all too many Christians yield to that pressure.

But Daniel and his companions refused to compromise with the pagan world and its allures. The glitz and glamour of the secular world may blind a person temporarily. But when the intoxication of sin wears off, we see the death and decay that lies just beneath the surface. Sin doesn't reveal its hard, destructive edge immediately—but the edge is there. We need to maintain our spiritual sensitivity, our obedience to God, so that we will not be taken in by the lures of this dying world.

Who is influencing whom?

A man once said to me, "I have a coworker who automatically assumes that I believe what he believes about God. He assumes that we belong to the same political party and that we want the same things from our government officials. He's 100 percent wrong, but I've discovered something important about myself. The reason he believes these things is because I have never said anything to challenge him. He constantly tries to influence me, but I have not been influencing him."

"What do you think would happen if you spoke up in response to his comments?" I asked. "Or better yet, what if you stated your beliefs first?"

"He'd probably think I'm weird. He'd probably tell others in the office that I'm a wacko. I could probably expect to hear a lot of snide comments from him in the future."

"And what would you do then?"

"I never thought about it. I suppose I could ask him why he's so sure he's right and I'm wrong. I could ask him for the evidence to support his opinion and give him the evidence that supports mine."

That was an excellent answer! As Christians, we are called to challenge the status quo. We are called to challenge the "politically correct" belief system—which, of course, is not correct at all. We are called to challenge individuals, institutions, and belief systems that do not exalt the Lord Jesus Christ.

As the apostle Peter wrote, "but in your hearts honor Christ the Lord as holy, always being prepared to make a defense to anyone who asks you for a reason for the hope that is in you; yet do it with gentleness and respect" (1 Peter 3:15-16a). So make sure you know what you believe—and why. Dive into God's Word and prepare yourself to defend God's truth.

Unfortunately, all too many Christians, eager to maintain favor with their worldly friends, tend to roll over and play dead. Instead of making a defense of the Christian hope that is in us, we clam up, turn red with embarrassment, and collapse. The worldly people around us are certainly not embarrassed or hesitant to give you their opinion—or to criticize yours. Why are we, who believe in a godly way of life and Christian morality, so shy about exercising our moral authority and challenging the status quo? Why do we shrink back from asking, "What is so good about your non-Christian, secular belief system? The Christian belief system leads to inner peace, a sense of purpose, and joy and satisfaction in serving God. My beliefs lead to a life that has great potential for genuine fulfillment, forgiveness, and eternal life. What does your belief system offer to compare with that?"

If you were to speak up and share your beliefs with the people around you, what is the worst that would happen to you? Well, you might be ridiculed and mocked. You might lose friends. You might even find that your unbelieving boss will start to persecute you and even deny you a raise or promotion.

When Daniel and his friends challenged the status quo, they risked death by torture—yet the threat of pain and death did not deter them from saying what needed to be said and doing what needed to be done. They refused to be silent. They spoke truth to power at great personal risk.

What is true?

The Bible tells us that these young men were chosen because of their intelligence and ability, and they were placed in a rigorous three-year course of study. They would have scored 1600 on the SAT and 150 on an IQ test. They were (as Daniel 1:4 tells us) "skillful in all wisdom, endowed with knowledge, understanding learning, and competent to stand in the king's palace." And they were to be taught "the literature and language of the Chaldeans."

What was this "literature and language of the Chaldeans"? And who were the Chaldeans? The Chaldeans were a subgroup of the Assyrian people, and their region had been conquered by the Babylonians. The Chaldean people have a longstanding reputation for their occult spirituality, their sorcery, and their astrological knowledge. They told mythological stories with veiled spiritual meanings. They acted as if they possessed a deep, hidden knowledge of the occult arts, and they offered their so-called wisdom to the Babylonian rulers in exchange for status, privileges, and a promise of safety.

The superstitious Babylonians weren't altogether sure if the Chaldeans truly possessed the magical powers they claimed, but why take a chance? So they went along with the Chaldeans—just in case. The Chaldeans were the power behind the Babylonian throne. They were the spiritual gurus who influenced the Babylonian emperor and the other lesser rulers and authorities of the land.

The literature of the Chaldeans told of the power of their many false gods. Daniel and his friends understood the language and literature of the Chaldeans, even though they did not believe in it. It was a literature of the supernatural, filled with stories of gods and goddesses and heroes and their many powers. The Chaldean literature gave instructions in the formulation of potions and the performance of rituals. Daniel and his friends were fed a diet of lies in the guise of education—much as many students today are being fed lies in their university courses. Then, as today, students want to know:

- What is true?
- Does God exist and what is he like?
- What is the meaning of life?
- What are the rules for success and reward?

In Israel, these young Hebrews had been taught that God's Word is true, that God does exist, that he is one God, that he is a God of justice and mercy, that the meaning of life is knowing him, and that the rules for success and reward are to love and obey him. But when these young Hebrews were exiled to Babylon, they were told a different set of rules: truths can be found only in hidden (occult) knowledge; there are many gods and they are capricious and unknowable; life has no meaning; and the rules for success demand that you seek occult knowledge and power.

If all this sounds familiar to you, it's because these same false rules are being taught in our schools and universities today. Wherever ungodly people are allowed to set the agenda for education, they always teach that truth is relative and can be understood only by a select few who have found the insider information. Ungodly people will always present a world in which nothing is truly reliable or lasting. They will present a world in which the God of the Bible is irrelevant and his truth is no longer needed or wanted.

When you are persecuted

Godly people believe in absolute truth. They understand that God's laws are absolute and unchanging because God himself is absolute and unchanging. They understand that we are all sinners in need of redemption and that only through God can we find forgiveness. The meaning of life can be found only by worshipping God and obeying his commandments. And as we worship him, he fills our hearts with an active love for one another.

King Nebuchadnezzar thought he could brainwash these young Hebrew men into accepting the Babylonian religion and way of thinking. He placed these four young men under the authority of the chief of the eunuchs, and the chief put them through a three-year crash course in Babylonian ideology and culture. But Daniel and his friends never lost sight of the fact that their teachers were ungodly men, steeped in pagan religion. They never forgot that the language and literature of the Chaldeans was rooted in their evil religious practices.

Above all, Daniel and his three friends never forgot that the God of Israel was the one true God. They never let go of their love for him or their obedience to him.

God calls us to pattern ourselves after these four Hebrew role models. When ungodly people ridicule Christ or the Christian faith, when they make statements about God or godly morality that are simply false and offensive, let's be polite yet firm. Let's challenge the status quo.

Politely ask, "Why do you believe what you just said? What is your basis for saying that? Why do you have such an intolerant view of my faith? The Lord Jesus Christ is my Friend and my Savior. Why do you think it's okay to mock and ridicule Someone who is so important to me?"

By asking these questions and challenging the ungodly status quo, you may plant seeds of truth that the Holy Spirit can use to help genuine faith bloom in that person's life. You may prompt that person to ponder questions and ideas that he or she has never considered before. So before you speak, always ask the Holy Spirit to give you wisdom and the right words to speak.

Don't expect people to change their minds on the spot. It may take days or weeks for them to change their opinion—and they may *never* change their opinion. What's more, the people you challenge may actually begin to despise you and persecute you even more. They may come up with new names to call you, new arguments to throw at you, and new ways to attack you. And that's okay! As Jesus told us:

> "Blessed are those who are persecuted for righteousness' sake, for theirs is the kingdom of heaven.
>
> "Blessed are you when others revile you and persecute you and utter all kinds of evil against you falsely on my account. Rejoice and be glad, for your reward is great in heaven, for so they persecuted the prophets who were before you" (Matthew 5:10-12).

And the apostle Paul reminds us, "Indeed, all who desire to live a godly life in Christ Jesus will be persecuted" (2 Timothy 3:12). So when you are mocked and persecuted for challenging the status quo and sharing the gospel of Jesus Christ, wear your persecution as a badge of honor and obedience to Christ.

3

Experiencing
God's Rewards

Daniel 1:10-21

I have never met a college student who truly liked cafeteria food—at least, not after the first couple of weeks. The four Hebrew students studying at the College of King Nebuchadnezzar, however, must have been in a special category. The food they were offered was the finest in the land, the same cuisine offered to the king himself.

King Nebuchadnezzar had established a rigorous academic program for his captive students from various conquered nations. The three-year course of indoctrination included courses in mathematics, science (with an emphasis in astrology), geography, political science, Babylonian literature, Babylonian history, and Babylonian religion. Daniel and his friends learned the rituals, traditions, and beliefs of the Chaldeans and Babylonians.

One of the most important incentives the Babylonians used to keep their captive scholars from rebelling was an array of royal luxuries, especially luxurious foods. The Babylonians believed that a strong body was essential to the functioning of a healthy mind. So the scholars of King Nebuchadnezzar's College were expected to remain in top athletic form so that they would display not only the mental prowess but the physical stature associated with leadership in the Babylonian culture.

Just as athletes in colleges today receive a special diet of enjoyable foods rich in protein for strong muscles and complex carbohydrates for energy, the captives in Babylon feasted on a diet that was vastly superior to that of the average Babylonian citizen. King Nebuchadnezzar and the chief of the eunuchs taught these young captives how to appreciate the best of everything. They learned to eat and drink like leaders and aristocrats, not commoners.

The problem for the four Hebrew captives was that the Babylonian foods were not kosher. The Babylonian chefs prepared foods that were not in keeping with the dietary laws God had commanded Israel to obey. The next passage in Daniel tells us how Daniel and his friends reacted to the pagan cuisine:

> [A]nd the chief of the eunuchs said to Daniel, "I fear my lord the king, who assigned your food and your drink; for why should he see that you were in worse condition than the youths who are of your own age? So you would endanger my head with the king." Then Daniel said to the steward whom the chief of the eunuchs had assigned over Daniel, Hananiah, Mishael, and Azariah, "Test your servants for ten days; let us be given vegetables to eat and water to drink. Then let our appearance and the appearance of the youths who eat the king's food be observed by you, and deal with your servants according to what you see." So he listened to them in this matter, and tested them for ten days. At the end of ten days it was seen that they were better in appearance and fatter in flesh than all the youths who ate the king's food. So the steward took

away their food and the wine they were to drink, and gave them vegetables (1:10-16).

Daniel was undoubtedly impressed with the array of food presented to him. Though he and his friends were captives, they enjoyed a privileged status in this land because of their intellectual ability. All around them, the captives of other conquered nations accepted these luxurious bribes and willingly cooperated with their masters. The pressure to conform was intense. The rewards for conforming were seductive. It would have been so easy to say yes.

But Daniel and his friends said no.

Christians today, both young and old, face similar temptations. We live in an era of unparalleled luxury, convenience, and pleasure. It would be easy to say yes to the temptations of our culture. It takes a great deal of faith, obedience, and character to say no to the enticing evil that is on our movie screens, TV screens, computer screens, and smartphones. It takes reliance on God to reject the temptations presented to us in the workplace and in the power structures of our world. The pressure to conform is intense.

That's why Paul, in his letter to the Romans, writes, "Do not be conformed to this world, but be transformed by the renewal of your mind, that by testing you may discern what is the will of God, what is good and acceptable and perfect" (Romans 12:2).

And that's why Jesus said in his high priestly prayer before going to the cross, "I have given them your word, and the world has hated them because they are not of the world, just as I am not of the world. I do not ask that you take them out of the world, but that you keep them from the evil one. They are not of the world, just as I am not of the world" (John 17:14-16).

Don't be conformed to the mold of this world. Break the mold. Say no to the world. The only way to say no to the world is by saying yes to God.

Called to be peacemakers

The Bible tells us that Daniel "resolved that he would not defile himself" (1:8) with the enticements and temptations of the Babylonian kingdom. What was wrong with the food of the Babylonians? It wasn't merely that the foods were ceremonially unclean or that they were unhealthy foods, such as fatty meats or the meat of unclean animals. These foods had been defiled by being offered to the Babylonian idols. The pagan people of the ancient world ate the leftovers of foods sacrificed to the pagan demon-gods. Eating those foods was an act of identification with the pagan gods. It was an act of worship. Daniel, Hananiah, Mishael, and Azariah could not eat the food of the gods because that would mean partaking in idolatry.

Instead, Daniel made up his mind to say a polite "no, thank you" to the foods offered to him and his friends. He resisted the authority of his Babylonian rulers, including the authority of King Nebuchadnezzar himself. But the way he chose to resist Babylonian authority is instructive to us all:

> "Test your servants for ten days; let us be given vegetables to eat and water to drink. Then let our appearance and the appearance of the youths who eat the king's food be observed by you, and deal with your servants according to what you see" (1:12-13).

Instead of simply refusing the Babylonian food, he politely suggested a test for a limited time—ten days. Then, he said, the chief of the eunuchs could make up his own mind which diet was healthier—the Hebrews' vegetable diet or the royal Babylonian diet.

The Bible tells us that, after ten days of eating only vegetables and drinking only water, Daniel and his friends "were better in appearance and fatter in flesh than all the youths who ate the king's food." Because they had passed the test that Daniel suggested, he and his friends were allowed to eat vegetables and drink water for the rest of their training program.

There is a lesson for us in Daniel's suggestion: Whenever you feel you must refuse an order from your boss or some other person in authority, try offering an alternative instead of simply saying no. Place a time limit on the test and let the authority figure know you are willing to be evaluated objectively. This shows that you're not simply being rebellious, you are offering a practical alternative, a "yes-yes" solution.

There is no indication that when Daniel refused to eat the food of his captors, he told them he was standing on religious principle. He never said, "Our religion forbids us to eat the unclean food that you wicked Babylonians eat." That would have been rude. He simply suggested an alternative, in keeping with the dietary laws that God had given to the Jewish people.

As Christians, we should never be ashamed to speak about our faith. We should never cover up or purposely hide our identification with Christ. But we do not need to be unnecessarily confrontational when dealing with non-Christian people. We don't have to turn every situation into an argument over religion. If we can address the situation from a practical standpoint, if we can offer a better solution to a problem, then there's no reason to start an argument.

That's one of the lessons of Daniel's solution to the question of what foods to eat. At all times, treat the ungodly with respect so that the Holy Spirit might have a greater opportunity to speak to their hearts about Jesus Christ. It's hard to win over someone when you are in the throes of a conflict. It's far more effective to influence others for Christ than to argue others into submission. By finding reasonable, practical solutions to the cultural differences and problems that arose, Daniel prevailed and earned the respect of those who had authority over him.

To influence our culture for Christ, let's find creative, practical alternatives to conflict. Sometimes conflict is inevitable, but we don't go looking for it. Whenever possible, seek peaceful solutions.

Don't accept the status quo

There's an old saying, "Come weal or come woe, my status is quo." In other words, no matter what happens, good or bad, I am opposed to change. That should never be a Christian's attitude. As Christians, we should never accept the notion that a situation cannot be changed. Christians are called to be agents of change. Our call as believers is to facilitate changed hearts, changed minds, and to alter the downward trajectory of our society.

Daniel saw himself as God's man in Babylon, God's agent of change in the pagan world. He refused to yield to pressure from his culture. Instead, he influenced the culture and forced *it* to change.

It's easy to stand up for God in a stadium full of fifty thousand other believers. It's a lot harder to stand up for God when you are the only believer in a room full of nonbelievers. It's a lot harder to stand up for God when godless people mock you and tempt you to do what is contrary to God's commandments.

God honors and rewards those who stand up for the truth and speak boldly for him. Jesus said, "So everyone who acknowledges me before men, I also will acknowledge before my Father who is in heaven, but whoever denies me before men, I also will deny before my Father who is in heaven" (Matthew 10:32-33).

God honored and rewarded Daniel for taking a bold and courageous stand for him in the land of Babylon:

> As for these four youths, God gave them learning and skill in all literature and wisdom, and Daniel had understanding in all visions and dreams (1:17).

Daniel demonstrated leadership ability by taking a courageous stand in obeying the Jewish dietary laws in spite of pressure to disobey.

So God rewarded Daniel and his companions with a gift of learning and skill in literature and wisdom. And God especially rewarded Daniel by giving him the ability to interpret dreams and visions.

If you are a Christian, you will be tested, you will be tempted, you will be pressured to compromise your integrity. Don't give up and don't give in. Don't make excuses. Maintain your obedience to God even when the heat is on.

In the book of Revelation, the angel said to the apostle John, "Blessed are those who are invited to the marriage supper of the Lamb" (Revelation 19:9). If you stand strong in the Lord and prevail against the pressure to worship at the table of false gods, you can be assured of a reserved seat at the marriage supper of the Lamb.

The knowledge God imparts

There's an important principle embedded in this passage: Daniel and his friends were given two distinct kinds of knowledge and understanding as a result of their obedience to God. Our Lord will do the same for you and me if we are obedient to him. The two kinds of knowledge God imparts are:

1. Knowledge of God's commandments. When you obey God, he rewards you first and foremost with increased understanding of his commandments. The more you obey him, the more you *want* to obey. Obedience to God becomes a habit, a way of life. Your desire to keep God's commandments grows every time you demonstrate your faithfulness to him.

When I was a young boy, I was allowed to do certain things, and I was not allowed to do other things. As with all young boys, my mind-set was: "When I grow up, I'm going to do the things my parents tell me I can't do, and nobody is going to tell me I can't!" The truth is, as I grew older, I discovered even more things I couldn't do! Why? Not because of my parents, but because God's Word told me I should not do them. And as I grew more mature in my faith, I wanted to do what is right—not because my parents made me obey, but because I had an ever-increasing desire to obey God.

2. Knowledge of the world. The Lord also rewards those who obey him with a deeper knowledge and understanding of the world. God gave these four young Hebrew scholars "learning and skill in all literature and wisdom." They were able to learn and understand the writings their captors presented to them—plus they had the added ability to discern what was right and wrong in the Babylonian literature. They knew how to apply what was good in Babylonian literature and disregard what was evil.

You and I desperately need a deep understanding of the world. So many theories, ideologies, and falsehoods are presented to us daily. These messages assault us in the media and assault our children in their classrooms. We need to be able to sift truth from falsehood. We need to be able to say, with conviction and authority, "That is true," "That is mere speculation," and "That's an outright lie."

These two forms of knowledge—knowledge of God's commandments and knowledge of the world—come primarily, if not exclusively, from God. He gives us this knowledge as a reward for obedience to his Word and his commandments. So the question that confronts us is this: What has God commanded us to do? What must we do to obey his commandments?

Daniel and his friends knew the Torah—the books of the Law of Moses—and they knew the writings of the prophets. Make no mistake about that. They had a deep understanding of God's Word. They had studied the Scriptures as boys. They may have been in Jerusalem for the purpose of taking their bar mitzvah exams when Babylon conquered the city. The priests of the temple in Jerusalem usually conducted those examinations, and those exams were far more rigorous and demanding than anything Nebuchadnezzar could impose on them.

To prepare for the Torah exams, boys of that age were expected to memorize large portions of the Torah, and some memorized the entire book (what we now know as the first five books of the Bible—Genesis, Exodus, Leviticus, Numbers, and Deuteronomy). Daniel and his companions undoubtedly knew the law, the writings of the prophets, and the book of Psalms—and they probably sang the psalms at every opportunity.

In addition, they were trained to live out the law in their everyday lives. The law governed what they ate, the feasts and holidays they observed, and the rituals they participated in. They didn't merely have knowledge of the commands of God. They had *life knowledge*. They had a depth of experience in obeying God's commands and worshipping him daily. They understood the concept of moral absolutes, because they lived by moral absolutes.

Why *vegetables*?

You may wonder why Daniel and his friends maintained a diet of vegetables while living in the king's palace in Babylon. What possible advantage could there be in eating only vegetables and drinking only water? But there were actually three important practical advantages. God always deals in the practical matters of life as well as the spiritual.

The first practical benefit of a vegetable diet is that *it helped these young men to think clearly*. The rich food and wine of the king's palace were likely loaded with sugar and fat. Babylonians offered such foods to the pagan gods because they were considered to be delicacies. But foods rich in fat and carbohydrates are not "brain food." From a nutritional standpoint, these foods will put you to sleep, not help you think. Imagine trying to study literature, science, history, philosophy, and religion after eating a huge Thanksgiving dinner! It can't be done. A Thanksgiving dinner makes you want to take a nap.

Feasting slows down our reasoning and fogs the memory. A stomach full of rich foods draws blood away from the brain, making you sleepy and less intellectually acute. So the vegetable diet that Daniel and his friends ate was designed by God to clear their minds and enable these young scholars to always be at their best. This vegetarian diet undoubtedly contained protein-rich foods like beans, lentils, nuts, and whole grains, so they could remain physically strong and mentally acute.

I'm not suggesting that you should convert to a vegan diet—and you should never radically alter your diet without consulting your doctor. But God told Daniel and his friends exactly what kinds of foods their minds and bodies needed, and that is what they obediently ate. The results spoke for themselves.

The second practical benefit of the vegetable diet was that *it gave these young men a clear conscience before God.* By eating only vegetables, Daniel and his friends knew they were in right standing with God because they were obeying him and putting him first. They didn't have the guilt feelings associated with foods that had been sacrificed to the pagan demon-gods of Babylon. Emotional and psychological baggage, such as guilt, can interfere with the thinking process. But a clear conscience leads to a clear mind.

People who are bound up emotionally or psychologically often lack mental and moral clarity. They are unable to see the wisest and most productive solutions to their problems. They don't know how to prioritize their actions or their spending. They can't reason clearly, and their decisions frequently prove disastrous. They keep making the same mistakes again and again because their judgment is clouded.

By obeying God's commandments and eating only vegetables, Daniel and his friends avoided the trap of guilt and remorse. They were free to use their brains to the best of their ability.

The third practical benefit of the vegetable diet is that *it increased their influence in Babylon.* After Daniel had won his point about eating only vegetables and drinking only water, he discovered that he could make other requests of his captors, and as long as his request was reasonable and lawful, his captors would cooperate.

This principle holds true in every situation. If you, as a Christian, believe that you cannot in good conscience do something your boss asks you to do, and you try to find a win-win solution, your boss will probably respect you for that. Moreover, your boss will be more likely to accommodate you in the future, because you went out of your way to accommodate him or her.

Daniel established a reputation as a young man who continually came up with solutions, innovations, and creative ideas. Then, as now, the person who thinks clearly, acts quickly, and demonstrates good judgment is the person who advances rapidly in the organization. That person usually becomes a Christian of influence.

The king's exam

After three years of intense study at the College of King Nebuchadnezzar, it was time for Daniel and his friends to take their final exam. The next few verses describe what that exam was like and how these four young men performed:

> At the end of the time, when the king had commanded that they should be brought in, the chief of the eunuchs brought them in before Nebuchadnezzar. And the king spoke with them, and among all of them none was found like Daniel, Hananiah, Mishael, and Azariah. Therefore they stood before the king. And in every matter of wisdom and understanding about which the king inquired of them, he found them ten times better than all the magicians and enchanters that were in all his kingdom. And Daniel was there until the first year of King Cyrus (1:18-21).

The chief of the eunuchs was obviously proud of these four Hebrew valedictorians. He himself went before the king and presented them to undergo the king's interrogation and examination.

King Nebuchadnezzar himself spoke with the four young men. His conclusion? Among all the scholars at the King's College, no other students were found who could compare with Daniel, Hananiah, Mishael, and Azariah. As a result, "they stood before the king"— they entered King Nebuchadnezzar's personal service.

Daniel and his friends faced King Nebuchadnezzar with total confidence and serenity. Standing in the presence of the king did not faze them one bit. They had become fluent in the Babylonian language, and they could discuss any issue with the king. No matter what subject they discussed, no matter what question the king put to them, Nebuchadnezzar found these young men to be ten times wiser and more knowledgeable than all the magicians and enchanters in Babylon. That's right—they were *ten times* more brilliant than the Chaldeans themselves!

What can we conclude from these verses?

First, we know that Daniel and his friends were able to think quickly, freely, and brilliantly. They knew all the facts. They had all the answers. They could supply all the solutions. They could think fast on their feet because they had clear minds, strong character, and years of preparation.

Second, we know that Daniel and his friends had nothing to hide. Each of them was an open book. When the king asked them questions, they didn't have to worry about the best way to shade the facts and make a good impression. They simply spoke the truth.

Many people today don't feel free to speak the truth. They have to ask themselves, "How should I answer this question? What can I say that won't get me into trouble? How did I answer this question yesterday? What sort of answer is this person looking for? What answer is the correct people-pleasing answer?" People who aren't free to speak the truth are miserable all the time. They live in fear of saying the wrong thing. Sometimes they stumble over their own lies and conflicting statements.

But those who have nothing to hide have nothing to fear. Those who seek the approval of God instead of the approval of men are free to speak what is true, right, and good. The truth really does set you free, as Jesus said.

Do you want to be free to speak the truth all the time? The place to begin is the point of obedience. When you commit yourself to absolute, continuous obedience toward God, you are free indeed.

4

Freedom from Fear

Daniel 2:1-19

Napoléon IV, Prince Imperial, was a grand-nephew and last heir of Napoléon Bonaparte. When the prince was about four years old, his family was vacationing at Biarritz, on the Bay of Biscay. The boy's father, Napoléon III, noticed that the prince seemed to be afraid of going into the water, so he picked up his son, carried him out into the sea, and tossed him into the waves. The boy struggled in the surf and finally clawed his way back onto the beach, sobbing and howling in fear.

His father picked up the prince and sternly tried to reason with him, ordering the boy to stop being afraid. The boy continued to cry.

"Why are you afraid of the ocean?" the exasperated father asked. "I've seen you stand without flinching while the soldiers fired their cannons. You weren't afraid then."

"That's because I'm in command of the soldiers," the little prince said. "I'm not in command of the sea."

Fear is common to us all. Some fears are natural. It's only reasonable to be afraid of walking out into traffic or touching a red-hot stove. But some fears are irrational and unrealistic. Those fears hold us back from becoming all that God meant us to be. God never intended us to live in a state of paralyzing fear. As Paul wrote to young Timothy, "For God gave us a spirit not of fear but of power and love and self-control" (2 Timothy 1:7).

In order for us to truly obey God and be his witnesses, his agents of change in a crumbling world, we must have the courage and boldness to speak up for God. We need to place our trust in him and have no fear of what our audience may think or say or do. Our courage comes from trusting God to fill us with his power and love and asking him to lead us in his plan so that we can walk in it.

A palace gripped by fear

One of the key themes in Daniel 2 is freedom from fear. As a reward for their obedience, God gave Daniel and his three friends, Hananiah, Mishael, and Azariah, a special ability to learn and understand. Their faithfulness gave them freedom from fear. As the chapter opens, the king has had a dream, and because of this dream, the entire palace has been thrown into chaos. The hearts of all who serve the king are gripped by fear:

> In the second year of the reign of Nebuchadnezzar, Nebuchadnezzar had dreams; his spirit was troubled, and his sleep left him. Then the king commanded that the magicians, the enchanters, the sorcerers, and the Chaldeans be summoned to tell the king his dreams. So they came in and stood before the king. And the king said to them, "I had a dream, and my spirit is troubled to know the dream." Then the Chaldeans said to the king in Aramaic, "O king, live forever! Tell your servants the dream, and we will show the interpretation." The king answered and said to the Chaldeans, "The word from me is firm: if you do

not make known to me the dream and its interpretation, you shall be torn limb from limb, and your houses shall be laid in ruins. But if you show the dream and its interpretation, you shall receive from me gifts and rewards and great honor. Therefore show me the dream and its interpretation." They answered a second time and said, "Let the king tell his servants the dream, and we will show its interpretation." The king answered and said, "I know with certainty that you are trying to gain time, because you see that the word from me is firm—if you do not make the dream known to me, there is but one sentence for you. You have agreed to speak lying and corrupt words before me till the times change. Therefore tell me the dream, and I shall know that you can show me its interpretation." The Chaldeans answered the king and said, "There is not a man on earth who can meet the king's demand, for no great and powerful king has asked such a thing of any magician or enchanter or Chaldean. The thing that the king asks is difficult, and no one can show it to the king except the gods, whose dwelling is not with flesh."

Because of this the king was angry and very furious, and commanded that all the wise men of Babylon be destroyed. So the decree went out, and the wise men were about to be killed; and they sought Daniel and his companions, to kill them. Then Daniel replied with prudence and discretion to Arioch, the captain of the king's guard, who had gone out to kill the wise men of Babylon. He declared to Arioch, the king's captain, "Why is the decree of the king so urgent?" Then Arioch made the matter known to Daniel. And Daniel went in and requested the king to appoint him a time, that he might show the interpretation to the king (2:1-16).

Nearly everyone mentioned in this passage is deathly afraid. King Nebuchadnezzar is afraid because he has had a frightening and disturbing dream. Upon waking, he finds he cannot remember the details of the dream. He remembers only the terror it instilled in him. So he calls his wise men together and demands that they tell him all the forgotten parts of his dream, then interpret the dream for him.

The so-called wise men have no idea what the king dreamed. The king's demand is unreasonable and irrational, yet if the wise men do not do as the king demands, he will tear them limb from limb and destroy their houses (that is, kill their families). It's a worst-case scenario, not only for these Chaldean wise men but for all the wise men of Babylon (2:12-13).

The fearless response of Daniel

Unlike the pagan wise men of Babylon, Daniel had a wisdom that comes only from God. So he "replied with prudence and discretion" to the captain of the king's guard. This captain had been sent out by the king to slaughter the Babylonian advisors, but Daniel stopped the king's captain with a question: "Why is the decree of the king so urgent?" So the captain explained the matter to Daniel, and Daniel averted the slaughter by sending a message back to the king: "I can interpret your dream." The Scripture narrative tells us what happened next:

> Then Daniel went to his house and made the matter known to Hananiah, Mishael, and Azariah, his companions, and told them to seek mercy from the God of heaven concerning this mystery, so that Daniel and his companions might not be destroyed with the rest of the wise men of Babylon. Then the mystery was revealed to Daniel in a vision of the night. Then Daniel blessed the God of heaven (2:17-19).

Daniel immediately huddled with his Hebrew teammates and he told them it was time to ask God for mercy and insight regarding this mystery. Only God could reveal the details of the king's dream—a dream that even the king himself could no longer recall.

So we see clearly that, when confronted with a crisis, Daniel's first instinct was to go to God in prayer.

Knowing God erases fear

Here we see yet another benefit to the obedience of Daniel and his companions. They did not merely understand the things of God; *they knew God personally.* They spoke to him and listened to him just as if they were speaking and listening to each other. To these four Hebrew scholars, God was not some impersonal force out in the cosmos. God was their personal friend. He knew them, and they knew him. There's nothing like knowing God in a personal way to assuage one's fear and anxiety.

Knowing God is not something you can learn from intellectual study. You can know God only by *experiencing* him, day in and day out, walking with him and talking with him and obeying his commands. Knowing God comes by prayer and by spending intimate quiet time with the Lord. It comes not only by talking to God but by listening to him speak within your heart and spirit. In this way, you truly come to know the fullness of what God has promised, what he expects of you, and what he has planned for your life.

I grew up in a Christian home, and I am eternally thankful that my parents raised me in the faith. I grew up hearing and knowing the stories of the Bible. I grew up memorizing passages of Scripture. I heard sermons that clearly presented the principles of God. I watched my family (both parents and older siblings) set an example of daily faithfulness to God. As a child and as a young man, I knew a lot about God.

But all of that was mere head knowledge, just information between my ears, until I came to *personally* know Jesus Christ as my Lord and Savior. Until I accepted what he did for me on the cross, until I asked him to forgive my sin and give me new life, God was just a concept to me, not a person. Only when I gave my heart and life to Jesus Christ did my relationship with him take on real meaning.

Before you accept Jesus as Lord and Savior, God seems remote—and even frightening. If you do not know God as your heavenly Father, you know him only as a Judge who has the power to punish you for your sin. And if you don't know him as your heavenly Father, you have reason to be afraid!

If you have never accepted Jesus as Lord and Savior, God's ways and purposes seem unknowable. But once you know Jesus personally, a light comes on. The unknowable becomes known. The mysterious becomes clear. Once you truly know him, you exchange the fear of wondering, *Have I done enough to please God?* for the peace and serenity of knowing that salvation is a free gift from a loving Father.

The first key to knowing God in a personal way is to obey God by accepting Jesus as Lord and Savior. Knowing him erases fear.

Prayer and faith: antidotes to fear

Daniel and his companions lived in Babylon about six hundred years before Jesus was born. At that time, the only way a young Hebrew man could know God was to obey God and be faithful in praying to him. This is how the Hebrew people built up a habit of trusting God.

The account in the book of Daniel doesn't tell us that Daniel and his friends met daily to pray and study God's Word. But we do know that at the first sign of trouble, these four friends dropped everything and went immediately to prayer. We can be sure that a person doesn't turn first to prayer unless prayer is already a daily pattern in his life. We know that when Daniel and his friends prayed, they clearly understood the attributes and nature of the One to whom they were praying. This kind of prayer comes only from those who truly know God in a personal and experiential way.

As we have seen, the Lord gave Daniel a special ability: "Daniel had understanding in all visions and dreams" (1:17). This was supernatural, spiritual knowledge about the ways God intervenes in human hearts. The truth of God's Word, from cover to cover, is that God reveals himself to people according to the steadfastness and consistency of their obedience. He entrusts those who obey him with a deeper understanding of his nature and his workings.

During their captivity, Daniel and his friends increasingly matured in their faith to a point where they were able to trust God with every aspect of their lives. Does this mean they never felt any fear or anxiety? No, it does not. We see that the king's edict drives these young men to their knees in prayer. They don't want to suffer and die—they want to live! The instinct of self-preservation is strong in all human beings, and that is why the thought of death makes us afraid. But these young men had a trust in God and an obedience toward God that was stronger than their fear. They were not devoid of fear, but their deep faith gave them victory over their fear. Faith overcomes fear.

The enemy of our faith is Satan, the devil. Why does Satan spend so much time trying to instill fear into us? He knows that those who are filled with fear are lacking in faith. In order to speak up for God's truth, we must have courage, faith, and a spirit of obedience. So Satan seeks to undermine our courage in order to silence our witness.

From my many years of studying the Bible, preaching the Word, and living the Christian life, I believe I have gained some insight into how the devil works. Before he tempts us, he seeks to undermine our confidence in God. He tries to confuse us. If we lack confidence in what we know about God, we easily become anxious and fearful. Those who lack knowledge of God's commandments and God's loving nature are easily led astray and have trouble thinking clearly.

Fearful people are always second-guessing themselves: "Is this the right thing to do? Will people criticize me if I speak the truth of God's Word? Will people reject me if I witness for him? Will God keep his promises to me? What if I speak boldly for God, but God does not defend me? What if God lets me down?"

When Satan is able to keep us frightened and confused, he is able to blunt our effectiveness for God. It's at that point that Satan often throws his strongest temptations at us. This satanic strategy is thousands of years old. The devil has been attacking human beings this way ever since the Garden of Eden. Why? Because it works! Satan goes after those who don't know God's Word, who don't obey God's commandments, and who lack a strong personal relationship with him. Satan uses lies to instill confusion and doubt. He causes us to question God's love and commandments.

When Satan succeeds in making us more concerned about pleasing people than pleasing God, when he makes us timid and reluctant to speak out for God, then he has won the victory over us. Fear has defeated faith, and Satan has silenced us.

Don't let fear overcome your faith. Grow deep in your faith so that you can overcome fear.

Steps to overcoming fear

In this section of Daniel, we see three steps for overcoming fear and curing spiritual confusion.

1. Know God's Word. If you want to overcome fear, you must look at reality from God's perspective. And the way to gain God's perspective on life is by reading and studying his Word. To see your life as God sees it, study his Word.

2. Grow deep in your relationship with God. It's not enough to know about God. You must know God in a deep and personal way. You grow in that relationship by learning and keeping his commandments, meeting with him daily in prayer, and quietly reflecting and meditating on his Word. As you pray, don't do all the talking. Spend time listening to the quiet voice of the Holy Spirit within you.

3. Develop a track record of trusting. You must learn to take risks for Jesus. Not foolish risks, like jumping off a cliff and asking God to catch you. No, I'm talking about daring to do great things and take on difficult challenges for God. I'm talking about daring to open your mouth and share the gospel with a neighbor. Or daring to get involved in a ministry to the poor and homeless. Or daring to host a Child Evangelism Good News Club in your home. Or daring to open your home to a young woman with a crisis pregnancy so that she can choose life for her unborn child.

There are risks to all of these actions. But God does not call us to play it safe. He calls us to obey him and trust him and to live out the gospel to everyone around us. God wants you to be strong in the faith, testing his promises and living free of fear. When you dare to do great things for God, you build a track record of trusting him. Every time you take a risk for him, and you see that he truly does keep his promises, your faith grows stronger. When faith is strong, fear evaporates.

Why did Daniel and his friends show no fear in meeting with Nebuchadnezzar? Everyone else in the palace was terrified. King Nebuchadnezzar had the power of life and death over every human being in the kingdom. Yet these four Hebrew teenagers took it all in stride. They didn't panic. They faced King Nebuchadnezzar with confidence and respect. Daniel, Hananiah, Mishael, and Azariah knew that Nebuchadnezzar could do nothing to them without permission from Almighty God.

The apostle Paul had the same confidence in the power of God in his life. As he wrote to the Christians in Corinth:

> For we do not want you to be unaware, brothers, of the affliction we experienced in Asia. For we were so utterly burdened beyond our strength that we despaired of life itself. Indeed, we felt that we had received the sentence of death. But that was to make us rely not on ourselves but on God who raises the dead. He delivered us from such a deadly peril, and he will deliver us. On him we have set our hope that he will deliver us again (2 Corinthians 1:8-10).

As you go through trials and afflictions, as you see God deliver you again and again in ways you never expected, your trust in him and your faith in him will grow. Does fear hold you back from taking a stand for Christ? Check your faith level. Check your prayer level. Check your obedience level. Start building a track record of trusting God in all things, great and small.

As you grow in your trust in God, you will see your fear begin to melt away. Someday, you may even find that you can stand before kings, speak God's truth, and not be afraid.

5

The Power of Praise

Daniel 2:19-49

In the spring of 1738, Charles Wesley lay in bed, struggling to breathe. He was going through a bout of pleurisy, an inflammation of the lining of the lung cavity. Every time he took a breath, the inflamed pleural linings rubbed against each other, causing extreme pain. He was suffering, he was depressed, and he was plagued by severe doubts about his faith.

One day, a group of believers came to his home in Bristol in southwest England. They prayed over him and cared for him. Wesley was deeply moved by their Christian love for him. He began to read his Bible, and found himself drawn again and again to the passages that dwelt on praise for God. He began to feel stronger, both physically and spiritually. He later looked back on his illness and recovery as the time his faith was renewed and restored.

The following year, Wesley was inspired to write an eighteen-stanza poem. It was set to music and published as a hymn in 1740. The original title was "For the Anniversary Day of One's Conversion."

Eventually, the seventh stanza was moved to the beginning of the hymn, and the first line of that stanza became the title it is now known by nearly three centuries later: "O For a Thousand Tongues to Sing." It is a hymn of exultant praise:

> O for a thousand tongues to sing
> My great Redeemer's praise,
> The glories of my God and King,
> The triumphs of His grace!
>
> My gracious Master and my God,
> Assist me to proclaim,
> To spread through all the earth abroad
> The honors of Thy name.

It was *praise* that lifted Charles Wesley from his sick bed, *praise* that renewed and restored his faith, and *praise* that he wrote about and sang about throughout the remaining years of his life.

Daniel's hymn of praise

In Daniel 2, Daniel and his friends faced a crisis that was every bit as discouraging, perilous, and frightening as Charles Wesley's crisis with pleurisy. These four young Hebrew exiles faced a death sentence from King Nebuchadnezzar. Their first response was to immediately drop to their knees and join their hearts in prayer. The biblical narrative discloses what happened after these four young men prayed together:

> Then the mystery was revealed to Daniel in a vision of the night. Then Daniel blessed the God of heaven (2:19).

This passage does *not* say that the mystery was revealed to Daniel in a dream. It says that the mystery was revealed to him "in a vision of the night." A vision is a very different experience from a dream. A dream is experienced during sleep. A vision is experienced while a person is awake—and often while that person is praying.

Immediately after God revealed the mystery to Daniel in a vision, Daniel responded with praise for God. The passage says, "Then Daniel blessed the God of heaven." Daniel didn't necessarily praise God for giving him the answer he asked for. He didn't necessarily praise God for giving him the words he needed to speak to King Nebuchadnezzar. He simply blessed God and praised him *for who he is.*

That is the essence of praise. We *thank* God for what he does and what he gives us. We *praise* him for who he is.

The instant Daniel received the revelation of the mystery of the king's dream, Daniel began his hymn of praise. The passage tells us:

> Daniel answered and said:
>   "Blessed be the name of God forever and ever,
>   to whom belong wisdom and might.
>   He changes times and seasons;
>   he removes kings and sets up kings;
>   he gives wisdom to the wise
>   and knowledge to those who have understanding;
>   he reveals deep and hidden things;
>   he knows what is in the darkness,
>   and the light dwells with him."
>   (2:20-22)

Notice that, up to this point, Daniel's hymn has been a song of pure praise. He blesses God and extols all the amazing qualities and traits of God. In the next verse, Daniel adds a note of thanksgiving to his chord of praise:

> "To you, O God of my fathers,
>   I give thanks and praise,
> for you have given me wisdom and might,
>   and have now made known to me what we asked of you,
>   for you have made known to us the king's matter."
>   (2:23)

Though praise is still a major theme of verse 23, Daniel adds his own personal gratitude to God, thanking him for giving him wisdom, power, and knowledge to deal with the king's troubling dream. Praise and thanksgiving are two different but closely related forms of prayer.

As Daniel gives thanks to God, he does not claim to have any wisdom or power of his own. Instead, he praises God as the source of all wisdom and power. The attitude of Daniel is so unlike that of people today, who claim they have achieved success, wealth, and power through their own ability. Nothing could be further from the truth.

You and I can accomplish nothing in life through our own power. It is God who gives us the health, intellect, resources, and opportunities to work and achieve. The Lord is worthy of our praise in all things. He is our Creator, Sustainer, Provider, Protector, and Ever-Present Help.

Daniel clearly understood this truth. "You have given me wisdom and might," he sang to God, "and have now made known to me what we asked of you." It's vital that we understand this truth as well.

Praise imparts power

God, the Source of all wisdom, had revealed the matter to Daniel. Only God himself could have known the forgotten portions of Nebuchadnezzar's dream. But it wasn't enough for Daniel to know the king's dream. He also needed the power and courage to *act* on that knowledge. So God imparted courage and power to Daniel so that he could stand confidently before the king.

You and I often know exactly what is needed to solve a certain problem. We know the solution—but the question is: Do we have the *courage* to do what needs to be done? Do we have the *power* to act? God gave Daniel not only the wisdom, but the boldness and power to act.

Praise to God imparts the power of God, and the power of God results in action. Praise connects you to God in a way that nothing else can. It points out to you, in the depths of your spirit, who God is—and who you aren't! You and I are not God, and we need to be reminded of that fact from time to time. Praise elevates God to his proper place in our thoughts while it knocks down our self-delusional pride.

When we gain a clear picture of who God is in relationship to us, when we realize that he has all the wisdom and power we need, then he delights in giving us a measure of his wisdom and power to use for his purposes. He desires the very best for your life—and the best for your life is that you act on what he gives you. When you see God answering your prayers and responding to your praise, you cannot help but be filled with awe and thanksgiving.

No matter how big the problem, God has the answer. No matter how difficult the trial, God can make a way when there seems to be no way. It doesn't matter how hopeless the circumstances seem, God can intervene.

There is power in the name of God and in the name of his Son, Jesus. God's Word tells us that the name of Jesus is above all names—including the name of any sorrow or tragedy we may face—Loss, Death, War, Disaster, Rejection, Prejudice, Accident, Cancer, Multiple Sclerosis, Alzheimer's Disease, Divorce, Abuse, Humiliation, Hunger, Bankruptcy, Poverty, Recession, or Depression. The name of Jesus is "far above all rule and authority and power and dominion, and above every name that is named, not only in this age but also in the one to come. And he put all things under his feet and gave him as head over all things to the church, which is his body, the fullness of him who fills all in all" (Ephesians 1:21-23).

When we praise the name of Jesus, we put things in their proper order. We declare to our own souls that we know who is truly in control of this world and all its problems. We declare to our own spirits that we know on whom we can rely for the answers and solutions we seek.

The awe and wonder we feel as we praise God and contemplate his greatness gives us a surge of confidence that nothing else can. God wants us to succeed, even when all the odds are against us. He wants us to experience his wisdom and power.

God is on our side.

Praise leads to joy, and joy produces strength

My grandfather, Oza, was a building contractor and a lay leader in the Brethren Church, to which my mother's family belonged. He lived in a small apartment adjacent to the home of my uncle. When I spent the night with my cousins, I would sometimes awaken at night to hear my grandfather praising the Lord in a loud voice.

I often wondered why my grandfather was so full of joy and praise to God. He had lost two sons when they were in their early thirties. He lost his wife while he was a relatively young man. Even so, until he died at the age of ninety-two, he never ceased to praise God throughout the night and again in the morning. It was praise, not life's circumstances, that gave my grandfather a heart full of joy and the courage to remain devoted to God in everything he did.

Praise to God brings joy and strength for everyday living. As the psalmists wrote:

> I love you, O LORD, my strength.
> The LORD is my rock and my fortress and my
>   deliverer,
>   my God, my rock, in whom I take refuge,
>   my shield, and the horn of my salvation,
>   my stronghold.
> I call upon the Lord, who is worthy to be praised,
>   and I am saved from my enemies.
>   (Psalm 18:1-3)

> Sing aloud to God our strength;
> shout for joy to the God of Jacob!
> (Psalm 81:1)

> The LORD is my strength and my song;
> he has become my salvation.
> (Psalm 118:14)

Again and again, the message of the Psalms is that those who make a habit of praise to God experience *joy*—and the joy of the Lord brings them God's salvation, deliverance, and protection. The more you praise God, the more confidence you feel, knowing you are connected to the King of the universe who hung the stars in space. The more you praise God, the more excitement you feel about what God is doing in your life; with him as your ever-present help, you cannot fail. The more you praise God, the more empowered you feel to take bold action, helping to spread God's love, truth, and justice throughout the world.

Praise empowered Daniel to go boldly into the presence of Nebuchadnezzar. Praise to God empowers you and me to go before the rulers of this earth with the message of repentance and salvation. Praise propels us to act. So spend time today praising God and declaring his glory. When you get up tomorrow, praise him again. Build a daily habit of praise to God. Praise him all day long. Praise him in every circumstance.

Praise empowers God's people.

Propelled into action

Praise empowered Daniel and launched him into action. The passage tells us what Daniel did next:

> Therefore Daniel went in to Arioch, whom the king had appointed to destroy the wise men of Babylon. He went and said thus to him: "Do not destroy the wise men

of Babylon; bring me in before the king, and I will show the king the interpretation."

Then Arioch brought in Daniel before the king in haste and said thus to him: "I have found among the exiles from Judah a man who will make known to the king the interpretation." The king declared to Daniel, whose name was Belteshazzar, "Are you able to make known to me the dream that I have seen and its interpretation?" Daniel answered the king and said, "No wise men, enchanters, magicians, or astrologers can show to the king the mystery that the king has asked, but there is a God in heaven who reveals mysteries, and he has made known to King Nebuchadnezzar what will be in the latter days. Your dream and the visions of your head as you lay in bed are these: To you, O king, as you lay in bed came thoughts of what would be after this, and he who reveals mysteries made known to you what is to be. But as for me, this mystery has been revealed to me, not because of any wisdom that I have more than all the living, but in order that the interpretation may be made known to the king, and that you may know the thoughts of your mind" (2:24-30).

Daniel went to the captain of the king's guard, the man who was ordered to slaughter all the wise men of Babylon, including the four Hebrew young men. Daniel told the captain not to carry out the slaughter but to take Daniel to the king. "I will show the king the interpretation," Daniel said. The captain hurried to Nebuchadnezzar and told him that Daniel would interpret the dream.

So Daniel came into the presence of the king.

King Nebuchadnezzar had been in a state of terror since experiencing the dream. He was unable to sleep. He was filled with anxiety and dread. But Daniel calmed his fears. He said, in effect, "This dream is a good thing. God has given you this dream so that you might know what is going to happen—and take action."

Daniel was also careful to give glory to God. He told King Nebuchadnezzar, "No wise men, enchanters, magicians, or astrologers can show to the king the mystery," but "there is a God in heaven who reveals mysteries." Credit belongs to God alone, said Daniel, not any human being. Then Daniel proceeded to tell the king what he had dreamed—and what the dream meant:

> "You saw, O king, and behold, a great image. This image, mighty and of exceeding brightness, stood before you, and its appearance was frightening. The head of this image was of fine gold, its chest and arms of silver, its middle and thighs of bronze, its legs of iron, its feet partly of iron and partly of clay. As you looked, a stone was cut out by no human hand, and it struck the image on its feet of iron and clay, and broke them in pieces. Then the iron, the clay, the bronze, the silver, and the gold, all together were broken in pieces, and became like the chaff of the summer threshing floors; and the wind carried them away, so that not a trace of them could be found. But the stone that struck the image became a great mountain and filled the whole earth.
>
> "This was the dream. Now we will tell the king its interpretation. You, O king, the king of kings, to whom the God of heaven has given the kingdom, the power, and the might, and the glory, and into whose hand he has given, wherever they dwell, the children of man, the beasts of the field, and the birds of the heavens, making you rule over them all—you are the head of gold. Another kingdom inferior to you shall arise after you, and yet a third kingdom of bronze, which shall rule over all the earth. And there shall be a fourth kingdom, strong as iron, because iron breaks to pieces and shatters all things. And like iron that crushes, it shall break and crush all these. And as you saw the feet and toes, partly of potter's clay and partly of iron, it shall be a divided kingdom, but some of the firmness of iron shall be in it, just as you saw iron mixed with the soft clay. And as

the toes of the feet were partly iron and partly clay, so the kingdom shall be partly strong and partly brittle. As you saw the iron mixed with soft clay, so they will mix with one another in marriage, but they will not hold together, just as iron does not mix with clay. And in the days of those kings the God of heaven will set up a kingdom that shall never be destroyed, nor shall the kingdom be left to another people. It shall break in pieces all these kingdoms and bring them to an end, and it shall stand forever, just as you saw that a stone was cut from a mountain by no human hand, and that it broke in pieces the iron, the bronze, the clay, the silver, and the gold. A great God has made known to the king what shall be after this. The dream is certain, and its interpretation sure" (2:31-45).

Daniel revealed the king's dream to him, a dream of a statue made of gold, silver, bronze, iron, and clay. Then a stone was cut out, but not by any human hands. It flew at the statue and smashed its feet of iron and clay. The statue crumbled into pieces, and the wind swept the pieces away. Daniel told the king this was a dream of future events.

An outline of future history

The golden head of the statue clearly represents the Babylonian Empire of Nebuchadnezzar, which lasted from 625 to 538 BC. The silver chest and arms of the statue represent a second empire, the Medo-Persian Empire, lasting from 539 to 330 BC.

The middle and thighs of bronze represent a third empire, Greece. This part of the statue probably referred to both the Greek Empire under Alexander the Great, 336 to 323 BC, and the Seleucid Empire that succeeded Alexander. The Seleucid kingdom was a vast Greek-Macedonian state that, at its height, stretched from Turkey in the west to Pakistan in the east.

The two legs of iron represent a fourth empire, Rome. A relatively weak Roman Republic had existed for more than five hundred years before Christ. But in 27 BC, the old Republic fell and was replaced by the iron-fisted Roman Empire under Julius Caesar. As the first of the Roman emperors, Julius Caesar transformed Rome into an expansionist, imperial power. As Daniel explains, this fourth empire would be "strong as iron, because iron breaks to pieces and shatters all things"—an apt picture of the power of the Roman Caesars.

The statue's two feet are made of a mixture of iron and potter's clay. Iron is strong, clay is weak, and the two cannot be bonded together. The result is that the feet of the statue were "partly strong and partly brittle." The feet probably represent Western civilization—the collection of powerful nations and cultures that were once under the domination of the Roman Empire.

Western culture includes the European nations, Great Britain, and the nations of the Americas and Australia that were settled by European nations. If this is an accurate interpretation, then the feet of iron and clay probably represent the culture and the times we live in today. Even now, we see that our once-dominant Western culture and economy are in decline. The economic and cultural dominance of the West may be coming to an end, as Daniel foretold.

Daniel goes on to tell the king, "And in the days of those kings the God of heaven will set up a kingdom that shall never be destroyed, nor shall the kingdom be left to another people. It shall break in pieces all these kingdoms and bring them to an end, and it shall stand forever" (2:44). This, of course, can only be the kingdom of God, the kingdom Jesus spoke of when he taught us to pray:

"Our Father in heaven,
hallowed be your name.
Your kingdom come,
your will be done,
on earth as it is in heaven."
(Matthew 6:9-10)

This future kingdom, Daniel says, shall never be destroyed and shall never be inherited by or conquered by another people. The kingdom of God will destroy all other earthly kingdoms, and it shall stand forever. This is the kingdom Jesus spoke of before Pontius Pilate: "My kingdom is not of this world" (John 18:36).

What is the stone that was cut from a mountain by no human hand, the stone that shattered the kingdoms of gold, silver, bronze, iron, and clay? That stone is Jesus himself. We know this because the stone was not cut by human hands. This stone came from God, and it grew to fill the whole earth. This speaks of all those around the world who know Jesus and have received him into their lives.

Throughout Scripture, Jesus is depicted by the metaphor of a stone. Jesus said we should build the "house" of our lives on "the rock" of Christ (Matthew 7:24-25). Paul calls Jesus the stone of Zion that is a rock of offense to unbelievers (Romans 9:33), but which produces a spring of refreshment for believers (1 Corinthians 10:4). And Peter, paraphrasing Psalm 118:22, states that Jesus, the stone the builders rejected, has become the cornerstone of history and of our salvation (Acts 4:11).

Jesus is the stone that strikes the feet of iron and clay, smashing all the empires and kingdoms of history. He overthrows all works of human pride and arrogance. This prophecy is as yet unfulfilled. It will take place when the Lord returns to establish his kingdom—a kingdom that will have no end.

The Lord's coming kingdom is referred to in both the Old and New Testament:

> "You shall break them with a rod of iron
>   and dash them in pieces like a potter's vessel."
>   (Psalm 2:9)

> "The one who conquers and who keeps my works until
> the end, to him I will give authority over the nations,

and he will rule them with a rod of iron, as when earthen pots are broken in pieces, even as I myself have received authority from my Father" (Revelation 2:26-27).

And then the lawless one will be revealed, whom the Lord Jesus will kill with the breath of his mouth and bring to nothing by the appearance of his coming (2 Thessalonians 2:8).

Then the seventh angel blew his trumpet, and there were loud voices in heaven, saying, "The kingdom of the world has become the kingdom of our Lord and of his Christ, and he shall reign forever and ever" (Revelation 11:15).

Daniel's concluding words to Nebuchadnezzar are: "A great God has made known to the king what shall be after this. The dream is certain, and its interpretation sure" (2:45). Because this dream and its interpretation came directly from God, this prophecy will take place. It is sobering to realize that parts of this dream have already been fulfilled, other parts will be fulfilled in the future—and some parts of this dream may be coming to fruition even as you read these words.

Facing our own Nebuchadnezzars

This passage of Scripture can be applied to our lives in more than one way. Not only is this a prophecy outlining events in human history, but the scene in which Daniel explains this prophecy to King Nebuchadnezzar is a lesson for us in how to respond to the troubled people in our lives.

King Nebuchadnezzar was a deeply disturbed man. In spite of all his power, we can see that he was insecure and filled with anxiety. Yes, he was a threatening figure, a man who wouldn't hesitate to use his power to destroy anyone who displeased him. He was, in short, a bully. But God had given Daniel wisdom in how to handle this bully. God gave Daniel insight into *why* King Nebuchadnezzar acted the way he did. He revealed to Daniel hurt and insecurity within King Nebuchadnezzar—and Daniel used this insight to deal with the king in a way that saved many lives, including his own.

We can draw a lesson for our own lives from Daniel's actions. Who is the difficult, threatening person in your life? Ask God to show you what he wants you to do. Ask him to give you insight into the emotional wounds and insecurities of that person. Ask him to give you words of healing power to speak to that person.

In the Sermon on the Mount, Jesus said, "But I say to you, Love your enemies and pray for those who persecute you, so that you may be sons of your Father who is in heaven. For he makes his sun rise on the evil and on the good, and sends rain on the just and on the unjust. For if you love those who love you, what reward do you have? Do not even the tax collectors do the same?" (Matthew 5:44-46). And Paul wrote, "Do not be overcome by evil, but overcome evil with good" (Romans 12:21).

So instead of repaying evil for evil and thinking of ways to get even with that person, ask God for the Christlike grace to love that person as Jesus would love him. Try to look past the irritation and provocation of that person's personality, and see the hurt, insecurity, and need in that person's life. What looks to you like a threat may actually be an opportunity for witness and ministry.

A friend once told me about a bullying personality she was dealing with at her office. Her supervisor was a cruel and verbally abusive woman who never missed an opportunity to dish out criticism and ridicule. The supervisor's behavior became so painful and destructive that my friend took a few days' retreat at a lakeside cabin for the sole purpose of praying for the situation. During this time of prayer and reflection, the Lord revealed to her that the supervisor had been suffering years of abuse, criticism, and ridicule from her own husband. The supervisor was starved for a positive word.

So my friend went to work on Monday morning with a game plan. She decided that every time her supervisor spoke abusively, she would look the supervisor in the eye and give her a positive reply—a word of appreciation for her skills, her appearance, and so forth. No longer would she simply cringe and slink off in resentment.

My friend told me, "The first time I did this, my supervisor just stared at me and made another critical remark, then turned and stomped away. But I refused to give up. The next time my supervisor criticized me, I again gave her a compliment—and again she gave me another critical shot, then stomped off. I refused to give up. The next time she criticized me, I replied with a compliment—and this time, she burst into tears. I was floored.

"At that point, I had an opportunity to tell her I was sorry for whatever was going on in her life that hurt her so much. From that day on, she never made another mean-spirited remark to me. Now I'm looking for opportunities to see if there might be some way I can help her and minister the love of God to her."

I can't guarantee that if you show kindness to the bully or tyrant in your life, you'll get the same results. The purpose of responding with Christlike grace is not to manipulate the other person into being nice. We are to behave in a Christlike way whether the other person ever responds positively or not. We are to obey the Lord and leave the results to him.

Activate the power

Daniel treated King Nebuchadnezzar with respect and Christlike compassion, and the outcome for Daniel was dramatic. Daniel 2 concludes with these words:

> Then King Nebuchadnezzar fell upon his face and paid homage to Daniel, and commanded that an offering and incense be offered up to him. The king answered and said to Daniel, "Truly, your God is God of gods and Lord of kings, and a revealer of mysteries, for you have been able to reveal this mystery." Then the king gave Daniel high honors and many great gifts, and made him ruler over the whole province of Babylon and chief prefect over all the wise men of Babylon. Daniel made a request of the king, and he appointed Shadrach, Meshach, and Abednego over the affairs of the province of Babylon. But Daniel remained at the king's court (2:46-49).

King Nebuchadnezzar literally prostrated himself before Daniel, the king bowing to the servant! The king honored Daniel, ordered that an offering and incense be presented to him, and made a profession of praise and awe to Daniel's God—the "God of gods and Lord of kings, and a revealer of mysteries."

Then the king promoted Daniel to an even higher position and showered him with gifts. Daniel became a governor over the province of Babylon, with authority over all of the king's wise men. At Daniel's request, the king appointed Shadrach, Meshach, and Abednego (Hananiah, Mishael, and Azariah) to serve as administrators over Babylon, the capital city.

What a dramatic transformation in the lives of Daniel and his three friends. The previous day, they had been under a death sentence. Now, they were the most powerful men in the empire, next to King Nebuchadnezzar himself.

What is the troubling situation that worries you right now? What pressures and threats do you face? Do you believe God is on your side? Do you believe he wants to turn the situation around for you?

We serve a powerful God. Our circumstances may not change as quickly as we would like, but God is on our side. He is working on our behalf. He is carrying out his eternal plan for your life and mine.

When you face a trial or a crisis, immediately go to prayer with your Christian friends. Praise God for who he is and for what he is going to do in your life. Ask him to act, to give you wisdom, and to give you boldness and courage. Ask him to use you to advance his kingdom.

Then thank him, and step out confidently, trusting God to work in ways that only he can work. Activate the power of prayer—and the power of praise.

6

Resisting Pressure and Temptation

Daniel 3:1-12

Elbert Hubbard was a writer and the founder of the Roycroft artisan community in East Aurora, New York. One of his most famous essays, "The Titanic," told the story of the 1912 sinking of the *Titanic*. Hubbard chronicled the last moments of a number of the *Titanic's* passengers, including department store magnate Isidor Straus and his wife, Ida. Mr. and Mrs. Straus were offered seats on one of the lifeboats, but Isidor courageously refused to board a lifeboat ahead of the other passengers, and Ida would not leave the ship without her husband. So Mr. and Mrs. Straus remained together on the sinking ship.

In his essay, Hubbard described the couple's courage and devotion, then concluded, "Mr. and Mrs. Straus, I envy you that legacy of love and loyalty left to your children and grandchildren. The calm courage that was yours all your long and useful career was your possession in death. You knew how to do three great things—you knew how to live, how to love, and how to die."[2]

Only three years after the sinking of the *Titanic*, Hubbard and his wife, Alice, boarded the liner RMS *Lusitania* in New York harbor. They were bound for Europe to collect stories about the World War in Europe—stories they planned to publish in their Roycroft publications. On May 7, 1915, eleven miles off the coast of Ireland, a German submarine torpedoed the *Lusitania* without warning. The ship sank in eighteen minutes, killing 1198 of the 1959 crew and passengers.

One of the survivors, Ernest Cowper, told the story of the last moments of Elbert and Alice Hubbard. Cowper was hurrying to a lifeboat with a small child in his arms when he saw the Hubbards standing arm-in-arm on the boat deck, gazing out to sea. Cowper stopped and asked them, "What are you going to do?"

They smiled and replied, "There doesn't seem to be anything to do." Then they turned and strolled back to their cabin, closing the door tightly behind them. Following the example of Mr. and Mrs. Straus, Mr. and Mrs. Hubbard knew how to live, how to love, and how to die. They faced life's most difficult test—and they passed it with character and courage.[3]

Life is filled with tests. You and I are tested again and again throughout our lives. I'm not talking about the kind of test the teacher gives you in school, or the kind of test that challenges your physical skills. The tests of this life are tests of character and courage. These tests rarely come when we feel strong and well prepared. They are the "pop quizzes" of life. They come when we least expect them. They hit us when we are weak, ill prepared, and at our worst. Yet they summon the best that is within us—our faith, our obedience, our boldness, and our willingness to trust God.

That is the kind of test that confronted Daniel's friends, Hananiah, Mishael, and Azariah in Daniel 3. When this test comes, these three young Hebrew leaders are known by their Babylonian names—Shadrach, Meshach, and Abednego. The test of their character and courage comes suddenly and unexpectedly:

> King Nebuchadnezzar made an image of gold, whose height was sixty cubits and its breadth six cubits. He set it up on the plain of Dura, in the province of Babylon. Then King Nebuchadnezzar sent to gather the satraps, the prefects, and the governors, the counselors, the treasurers, the justices, the magistrates, and all the officials of the provinces to come to the dedication of the image that King Nebuchadnezzar had set up. Then the satraps, the prefects, and the governors, the counselors, the treasurers, the justices, the magistrates, and all the officials of the provinces gathered for the dedication of the image that King Nebuchadnezzar had set up. And they stood before the image that Nebuchadnezzar had set up. And the herald proclaimed aloud, "You are commanded, O peoples, nations, and languages, that when you hear the sound of the horn, pipe, lyre, trigon, harp, bagpipe, and every kind of music, you are to fall down and worship the golden image that King Nebuchadnezzar has set up. And whoever does not fall down and worship shall immediately be cast into a burning fiery furnace." Therefore, as soon as all the peoples heard the sound of the horn, pipe, lyre, trigon, harp, bagpipe, and every kind of music, all the peoples, nations, and languages fell down and worshipped the golden image that King Nebuchadnezzar had set up (3:1-7).

Nebuchadnezzar had commanded the construction of a giant monument honoring himself and his reign—an image of gold ninety feet high, standing on the plain of Dura in the Babylonian province, and visible from every corner of the city.

After the monument was completed, Nebuchadnezzar summoned the officials of the nation to a dedication ceremony. As the crowd stood in awe before the monument, a herald announced that, at the sound of a vast orchestra playing every kind of music, the people were to fall on their faces and worship the image. Anyone who did not obey the king's command would be thrown into a blazing furnace as hot as an iron smelter.

For the four young leaders from Israel, this was an extreme test of character and courage. It was one of those pop quizzes of life that came about unexpectedly—and the consequences were not merely pass or fail, but *life or death*.

The life-and-death test of Shadrach, Meshach, and Abednego

In Daniel 2, we saw that King Nebuchadnezzar was impressed when Daniel was able to tell him his dream, and then interpret it. The king actually fell on his face and paid homage to Daniel, saying, "Truly, your God is God of gods and Lord of kings, and a revealer of mysteries, for you have been able to reveal this mystery."

But here in Daniel 3, we see that while King Nebuchadnezzar was impressed by Daniel's God, he did not have a conversion experience. He was not moved to commit his life to the service of the Lord Most High. His heart was not changed. He remained self-centered and devoted to the glorification and deification of himself. In demanding that the people bow down and worship this image, Nebuchadnezzar was demanding that the people worship him.

In his arrogance, the king tested his people, and no one was exempt. There was no provision for excuses. Everyone was expected to worship the king, even if their religion forbade such a practice. And, of course, the law of God, which the Lord gave to Israel after delivering the Israelites out of Egypt, said:

> "You shall have no other gods before me.
> "You shall not make for yourself a carved image, or any likeness of anything that is in heaven above, or that

is in the earth beneath, or that is in the water under the earth. You shall not bow down to them or serve them, for I the Lord your God am a jealous God, visiting the iniquity of the fathers on the children to the third and the fourth generation of those who hate me, but showing steadfast love to thousands of those who love me and keep my commandments" (Exodus 20:3-6).

So King Nebuchadnezzar had placed Daniel and his companions in a no-win situation. It was unthinkable that they could ever disobey the law of God. But to obey God, these men of Israel would have to disobey the king—and the penalty for disobedience was a fiery death.

The king's commandment was quite specific. The leaders of the nation were to prostrate themselves before the monument and worship it. The act of falling facedown on the ground before the image was a sign of complete obedience to, and worship of, the rule and power of Nebuchadnezzar. It amounted to an active affirmation that there is no power greater and more glorious than Nebuchadnezzar. It was nothing less than worshipping the king as if he were God— an act of idolatry, betrayal, and blasphemy toward the God of Israel.

Most of those who gathered on the plain before the image were officials of the Babylonian Empire. Some of them were from other cultures and nations. Three of them were Jewish captives—Shadrach, Meshach, and Abednego.

The signal to the people that they were to bow and worship was *music*—a loud and majestic piece of music that was probably composed especially for this event. It might have been the national anthem of Babylon. The fact that so many instruments were involved suggests that the music needed to be audible a long distance away. Because the signal would be music, not a voice, even people who spoke other languages would not be exempt. There would be no excuse for failing to obey the signal.

The penalty for failing the test would be death by fire. There would be no trial, no defense attorney, no jury. Judgment would be instantaneous, and the death sentence would be carried out immediately.

The means of death is significant. Throughout the ancient world, people offered sacrifices to false gods, and those sacrifices were often burned in furnaces like the one in Daniel 3. In those brutal pagan cultures, people even tossed their own children alive into the fire as sacrifices to their demon-gods.

Nebuchadnezzar was saying, in effect, "Bow or burn. Whether you offer your worship willingly or the guards toss you bodily into the furnace, you will serve the image." By linking the ceremony for the image to a fiery sacrifice, King Nebuchadnezzar was not only making this monument a symbol of the government of Babylon, but he was also making it an idol, a false god. He was declaring himself to be not just an earthly king, but a deity worthy of worship.

This was the life-and-death test Shadrach, Meshach, and Abednego faced.

Turning temptation into a test

In the Bible, a test is often described as a temptation. A temptation is a test of our value system and our resolve to serve God in absolute obedience. The Bible makes it clear that God does not tempt his people:

> Let no one say when he is tempted, "I am being tempted by God," for God cannot be tempted with evil, and he himself tempts no one. But each person is tempted when he is lured and enticed by his own desire. Then desire when it has conceived gives birth to sin, and sin when it is fully grown brings forth death (James 1:13-15).

Satan, who is also called the devil and the tempter, uses our desires against us, presenting to every person certain tests and temptations that are designed to make us fail. Satan's temptations are deliberately crafted to entice us into sin, which robs us of God's blessing in our lives. Sin blocks our relationship with God, harms our witness and our Christian reputation, hinders our prayer life, and can even cause physical harm and death.

Satan presents his temptations to us not only as enticements to physical pleasure, but also as trials and difficulties to cause us to doubt the goodness and love of God. Satan will throw any stumbling block in our way, anything to trip us up and tip us into spiritual discouragement. He wants us to question God, question his commandments, and sin against him.

But God can take the worst that Satan throws at us and can turn it into blessing for our lives. God can take the temptation of Satan and turn it into *a test of our faith*. When we, in reliance on the power and Spirit of God, are able to pass that test and withstand the temptation, God's power is revealed to us in a new and exciting way. By saying no to temptation and yes to God, we pass the test and reveal God's active presence in our lives. God's Word promises wonderful blessings for us when we overcome temptation. The apostle James puts it this way:

> Count it all joy, my brothers, when you meet trials of various kinds, for you know that the testing of your faith produces steadfastness. And let steadfastness have its full effect, that you may be perfect and complete, lacking in nothing...Blessed is the man who remains steadfast under trial, for when he has stood the test he will receive the crown of life, which God has promised to those who love him (James 1:2-4,12).

The end result of overcoming a temptation is blessing. When we overcome temptation we become more mature, more fulfilled, more confident, and better prepared for future service and success. God promises heavenly rewards to those who remain steadfast in the face of trials and temptations. When Satan throws a stumbling stone at us, God uses it as a building block.

Satan used the arrogant pride and murderous threats of King Nebuchadnezzar to tempt the officials of Babylon, including Shadrach, Meshach, and Abednego. But God had a plan for turning temptation into testing and for unleashing tremendous blessing in the lives of the three young men who passed the test.

How to pass the test

How do we apply the test of Nebuchadnezzar to our lives? As we examine the story, there are at least four specific, practical applications we can make to our daily experience.

1. No one is immune to temptation. In our culture, temptation is forced on us from every side. Our society actively pressures us to sin. You cannot drive down the street, turn on your radio or television, pass by a grocery store magazine rack, or enter a movie theater without facing messages designed to move you closer to sin. The notion of sinning may be the furthest thing from your thoughts. You could be praying, singing hymns, or on your way to a Bible study, when suddenly an advertisement or a book cover catches your attention and tempts you to sin.

It doesn't matter how long you have been a Christian or how strong your commitment to Christ. You can and will be tempted from time to time—and temptation will often pop up suddenly, without warning, and hit you when you least expect it. There is no vaccination for temptation.

2. False gods and idols are all around us. We live in an Internet age, the techno-savvy twenty-first century, and we think idol worship is an ancient superstition. But that is an illusion. We are still surrounded by idols today, though we don't recognize them. That's because we don't understand what an idol really is. An idol doesn't have to be a statue of a god made of metal, stone, or wood. An idol is anything we put our trust in. It is even possible for Bible-believing Christians to have idols—things that they trust in for their security, provision, or fulfillment, things that take the place that should be occupied by God alone.

When God commanded the Israelites, "You shall have no other gods before me," he was also saying, "When I look out over the camp of the Israelites, I don't want to see any gods before my eyes. I don't want to see them hidden in your tents or garments. I don't want to see you trusting in anything or anyone other than me for your security, provision, or fulfillment."

Where have you placed your trust for the future? Your investments? Your 401(k)? Your gold? The Social Security system? A president or a political party? An ideology?

Where have you placed your trust for happiness? Your spouse? A friend or family member? Your status? Your wealth? Your social circle? Your church? Your possessions?

Where have you placed your trust for your health? Your doctor? Your HMO or insurance plan? Your exercise regimen? Your diet? Your vitamins and nutritional supplements?

Where have you placed your trust for your identity? Your career? Your family? Your children or grandchildren?

Trust is a big issue to God. Whatever we trust *that is not God* is an idol. God spoke through the psalmist David:

> And those who know your name put their trust in you,
>   for you, O Lord, have not forsaken those who
>   seek you.
> (Psalm 9:10)

> I hate those who pay regard to worthless idols,
>   but I trust in the Lord.
> (Psalm 31:6)

And God spoke through wise King Solomon, who wrote in the book of Proverbs:

> Trust in the LORD with all your heart,
>   and do not lean on your own understanding.
> In all your ways acknowledge him,
>   and he will make straight your paths.
>   (Proverbs 3:5-6)

When we devote ourselves to something other than God, when we place our trust and invest our identity in status, wealth, career, possessions, health, politics, and similar pursuits, we may not think we are engaged in idol worship, but that's because we misunderstand what it means to worship. To worship is to serve. Worship is an act of obedience. When we put our trust in something other than God, we are serving an idol.

Suppose you have a home at the lake, a place to visit on weekends. The home needs maintenance, and so does the boat and the boat dock. Well, you work hard all week. Often the only time left for fixing up the place at the lake is the weekend. So, come Sunday morning, where are you? Are you worshipping God—or serving your idol at the lake?

Or suppose you have an IRA account that you are trusting to take care of you in your old age. During your working years, you are serving that IRA. How? With automatic withdrawals from your paycheck. You could also arrange for automatic withdrawals from your paycheck for your tithes and offerings, but the very suggestion rubs you the wrong way. Could it be that serving your IRA is more important to you than worshipping God with your tithes and offerings?

Or consider a person who works out daily at the gym. He is trusting in his physical fitness to keep him alive longer and to maintain his health. He goes faithfully to the gym every night after work. His fitness level needs daily servicing. But what happens when he comes home from the gym on Wednesday evening? Is he too tired to attend the weekly Bible study? Is his spiritual health as important to him as his physical health? Is his relationship with God as important to him as the maintenance of his body? Who or what is he truly serving and worshipping?

No one is immune to the temptation of serving a false god or putting an idol before God. It is a danger we all deal with.

3. Sin is deadly. Satan is subtle. He doesn't come to you as bluntly as Nebuchadnezzar and say, "Do this or die." The devil is a deceiver, and his goal is to mislead you, just as he misled Eve:

> Now the serpent was more crafty than any other beast of the field that the Lord God had made.
>
> He said to the woman, "Did God actually say, 'You shall not eat of any tree in the garden'?" And the woman said to the serpent, "We may eat of the fruit of the trees in the garden, but God said, 'You shall not eat of the fruit of the tree that is in the midst of the garden, neither shall you touch it, lest you die.'" But the serpent said to the woman, "You will not surely die. For God knows that when you eat of it your eyes will be opened, and you will be like God, knowing good and evil" (Genesis 3:1-5).

Satan, in the guise of a crafty serpent, used several ruses to beguile the woman. He knew that God had not forbidden Adam and Eve to eat of any tree in the garden—just one. So he deliberately misstated God's command. He subtly planted doubt in Eve's mind regarding God's warning. "You will not surely die," Satan whispered in her ear. But God, in his Word, reminds us, "For the wages of sin is death, but the free gift of God is eternal life in Christ Jesus our Lord" (Romans 6:23). Satan still uses the same tactic today, planting doubt in our minds about God's Word and hiding the horrors behind the pleasing temptations he offers us.

Satan's lie usually goes something like this: "Your lusts, passions, and ambitions are only natural. It's healthy and normal to satisfy them. Don't be left out. Don't be unhappy, unfulfilled, and frustrated. You can have more pleasure, more fame, more power, more money, more sex, more happiness, more of whatever you want. Conform to the culture. Conform to the world. Conform to your desires and appetites and lusts. That's the way to be happy. How could anything that feels good be wrong?"

That's the temptation. That's the lie.

But that's also an opportunity to grow in your faith and in your trust relationship with God. If you resist the temptation, if you reject the lie, if you place your trust in God, you will pass the test. And you will truly *live*.

Stand tall and say *no*

When I was in my early twenties, I found myself in an environment hostile to all the principles and values I held to be true. I was tempted again and again to compromise my faith and my principles. The peer pressure was intense, and the only way I could stand against it was to say *no!* repeatedly and with conviction. I said *no* so often in such a short period of time that I developed a reputation for my emphatic *no*. Whenever the people around me heard someone say a definitive, conclusive, unambiguous *no*, they would say, "That's a Youssef no!" I meant what I said, and no one had any doubts about it.

Shadrach, Meshach, and Abednego said *no* to King Nebuchadnezzar and they said so with their actions alone:

> Therefore at that time certain Chaldeans came forward and maliciously accused the Jews. They declared to King Nebuchadnezzar, "O king, live forever! You, O king, have made a decree, that every man who hears the sound of the horn, pipe, lyre, trigon, harp, bagpipe, and every kind

of music, shall fall down and worship the golden image. And whoever does not fall down and worship shall be cast into a burning fiery furnace. There are certain Jews whom you have appointed over the affairs of the province of Babylon: Shadrach, Meshach, and Abednego. These men, O king, pay no attention to you; they do not serve your gods or worship the golden image that you have set up" (Daniel 3:8-12).

King Nebuchadnezzar said, "Bow down!" The music blared. Thousands of people fell on their faces and worshipped.

Three men remained standing, surrounded by a sea of prostrate worshippers. They stuck out like banjo players in a symphony orchestra. The music played on. The three men remained standing. Somewhere, men with black-smudged faces and cinders burned into their arms stoked a blazing hot furnace.

Shadrach, Meshach, and Abednego knew that a furnace was being fired up for them—yet they remained standing. They remembered how their friend Daniel had stood strong in the faith before King Nebuchadnezzar. On this day, Daniel was not with them, but they followed Daniel's example.

When you are tempted and pressured to serve false idols, say *no*. Say it every time. Say it with conviction. Say *no* even though everyone around you has fallen prostrate before the idol. Say *no* even if you're the only person standing.

No matter how this world, your society, and Satan himself might threaten and pressure you, stand firm, say *no*, and put your trust in God.

7

God Is with Us in the Fiery Furnace

Daniel 3:13-30

Rev. John G. Paton (1824-1907), was a Scottish Protestant missionary to the New Hebrides Islands in the South Pacific. He worked for many years among cannibal tribes and was often threatened with death. In his autobiography, published in 1891, Paton tells how he and his coworkers at the island mission station were threatened by a "fiery furnace" crisis.

After weeks of threats from surrounding tribesmen, Paton and his fellow missionaries were exhausted. They tried to always have someone awake during the night to keep watch against attacks. But fatigue finally caught up with them. All the missionaries in the mission house lay asleep.

At ten o'clock at night, John Paton's dog nipped at his clothes and awakened him. Paton got up, looked out the windows, and saw men surrounding the mission house. He quietly awoke his fellow missionaries, Mr. and Mrs. Mathieson, and they prayed together, asking for God's protection.

As they prayed, a glare of light flickered through the windows. John Paton looked out and saw islanders with flaming torches passing the mission house. The attackers went to the church building nearby and set it aflame. Then they torched a fence made of dry reeds. Paton knew the flames were burning along the fence toward the mission house. The islanders were waiting to ambush them as they ran out to escape the flames.

John Paton grabbed an unloaded revolver and headed for the door to confront the attackers, ignoring Mr. Mathieson's attempt to stop him. "Let us die together," Mathieson pleaded. "You'll never return!"

"Leave that to God," Paton replied. "In a few minutes our house will be in flames. Then nothing can save us." And he went outside.

While Mr. and Mrs. Mathieson prayed inside the house, Paton ran to the burning reed fence and tore it apart to make sure the fire wouldn't reach the mission house. As he fought the flames, Paton realized he was surrounded. Seven or eight island men stood around him, clubs raised. One shouted, "Kill him!"

Paton raised the empty revolver and pointed it at the first man who moved, whispering an urgent prayer to God. Then he said in the island language, "If you strike me, Jehovah God will punish you. He protects us and will punish you for burning his church. We love you all—and you want to kill us for doing only good to you. But God is here now to protect us."

In his autobiography, Paton recalled what happened next: "They yelled in rage, and urged each other to strike the first blow, but the Invisible One restrained them. I stood invulnerable beneath His invisible shield, and succeeded in rolling back the tide of flame from our dwelling-house."

In the next moment a whirling wind rose up, filled with a pounding rain. "The wind bore the flames away from our dwelling-house,"

Paton wrote. "It had become almost impossible now to set fire to our dwelling-house."

The islanders were thunderstruck. They lowered their clubs and said to each other, "That is Jehovah's rain! Truly their Jehovah God is fighting for them and helping them!"

Gripped by panic, the attackers discarded their torches and scattered, disappearing into the bush. "I was left alone," John Paton concluded, "praising God for His marvelous works. 'O taste and see that God is good! Blessed is the man that trusteth in Him!'" That night, John Paton and the Mathiesons held a prayer and praise meeting. They had been protected and delivered from a fiery trial by the hand of God.[4]

He is present in our fiery trials

Down through the ages, God has not changed. He delivered his people from fiery trials in Old Testament times, and in the New Hebrides Islands in the late nineteenth century—and he is still delivering his people today. Even amid the flames of testing and trial, God is present with us. He will not let us down.

Daniel's protégés—Shadrach, Meshach, and Abednego—learned to experience the presence of God even in the most difficult hour of their lives. They experienced his presence in the midst of the burning furnace, and the reason God was present with them in their fiery trial was that they had maintained a close relationship with him.

Relationships take time to build. You cannot enter into the depths of a close friendship with God in the first few moments of your walk with him. The time to develop an intimate relationship with God is long before a crisis hits.

Shadrach, Meshach, and Abednego didn't have the privilege of asking Nebuchadnezzar to pause for a moment so that they could hold a prayer meeting. Once the music began to play, they had to make an instantaneous decision: bow down to an idol or stand up for God.

The pagans of the ancient world bowed low with their face in the dust to show deference to their false gods and cruel rulers. But the Jewish posture in prayer was the exact opposite. The Jews stood upright, arms raised from the elbow, palms open and facing outward. The high priest of the temple stood in this position before the Holy of Holies each day. A person standing before God with open and raised palms said, in effect, "Examine me, Lord. You'll see that I keep nothing back from you, and I rely on you for everything. Know me thoroughly, even as I desire to know you."

The people of Israel did not have to grovel or humiliate themselves before God. Rather, God invited them to come in all respect and humility and to enter into a relationship marked by direct communication.

When Shadrach, Meshach, and Abednego chose to remain standing, they sent a strong signal. They immediately placed themselves in the position of prayer as Hebrew people standing in the presence of Jehovah God. They would not place themselves in a position of groveling before pagan gods, as the Babylonians did. These servants of God undoubtedly cried out to him in silent prayer as they stood in defiance of the king's command.

Some of the Chaldean astrologers went to King Nebuchadnezzar and maliciously accused the three Hebrews, saying, "There are certain Jews whom you have appointed over the affairs of the province of Babylon: Shadrach, Meshach, and Abednego. These men, O king, pay no attention to you; they do not serve your gods or worship the golden image that you have set up" (3:12). The narrative of the book of Daniel shows us the king's reaction:

> Then Nebuchadnezzar in furious rage commanded that Shadrach, Meshach, and Abednego be brought. So they brought these men before the king. Nebuchadnezzar answered and said to them, "Is it true, O Shadrach, Meshach, and Abednego, that you do not serve my gods

or worship the golden image that I have set up? Now if you are ready when you hear the sound of the horn, pipe, lyre, trigon, harp, bagpipe, and every kind of music, to fall down and worship the image that I have made, well and good. But if you do not worship, you shall immediately be cast into a burning fiery furnace. And who is the god who will deliver you out of my hands?"

Shadrach, Meshach, and Abednego answered and said to the king, "O Nebuchadnezzar, we have no need to answer you in this matter. If this be so, our God whom we serve is able to deliver us from the burning fiery furnace, and he will deliver us out of your hand, O king. But if not, be it known to you, O king, that we will not serve your gods or worship the golden image that you have set up" (3:13-18).

Crying out to God

Throughout the Bible, and especially in the Psalms, God's people cried out to him for help, sustenance, deliverance, and strength. For example, in Psalm 107:19, the psalmist writes,

> Then they cried to the LORD in their trouble,
>   and he delivered them from their distress.

To cry out to the Lord means to come before him in complete vulnerability and dependency. There is no holding back, no putting on a brave face, no attempt to bargain with God. To cry before the Lord means to cast your entire self upon the Lord because you know from the core of your being that you cannot survive without him. It means that you come to God in an attitude of abject dependence, willing to express every emotion without holding back.

Clearly, God already knows how you feel. But when you cry out to him, *you* begin to realize how you feel. We often do not understand and appreciate our emotions until we express them in words, in tears, in groanings, in an honest and uninhibited display of our feelings before God.

You cannot cry out to God with a heart full of pride. You cannot cry out to God with an attitude of self-sufficiency. You can cry out to God only when you are so utterly dependent on him that there is almost nothing to say except, "Lord, help me!" If you cry out to God, he will answer. If you cry out for mercy, you will feel his forgiveness flooding your life. If you cry out for deliverance from fear and anxiety, you will feel his peace filling your soul. If you cry out in your loneliness and loss, you will feel his comfort and friendship in the depths of your spirit.

God always answers our deepest cries first with his presence, and then with his practical provision. He assures us that he is with us, he is for us, and he will act on our behalf—then he takes on our needs, our enemies, and our issues.

Shadrach, Meshach, and Abednego knew this to be true. They knew that God was present with them and that he would honor their obedience—whether or not he chose to deliver them from the furnace. When the music sounded and the entire nation bowed low, they stood tall.

Nebuchadnezzar had respected and admired these learned young Hebrews and had given them positions of great authority in his kingdom. He was undoubtedly stunned at their act of rebellion. Yet even in his fury, the king prized their wisdom and abilities so much that he was willing to give them a second chance. He told them that if they would simply fall down and worship the image he had made, all would be well. They would not be punished. "But if you do not worship," the king added, "you shall immediately be cast into a burning fiery furnace. And who is the god who will deliver you out of my hands?"

Shadrach, Meshach, and Abednego were filled with the presence of God. They replied firmly but respectfully, "Our God whom we serve is able to deliver us from the burning fiery furnace, and he will deliver us out of your hand, O king. But if not, be it known to you, O king, that we will not serve your gods or worship the golden image that you have set up."

The king is unnerved

King Nebuchadnezzar could hardly believe his ears. He was accustomed to being feared as an absolute dictator. People trembled in his presence, knowing he had the power of life and death over everyone in the empire. In all his life, no one had ever spoken to him as Shadrach, Meshach, and Abednego had spoken. Daniel records what happened next:

> Then Nebuchadnezzar was filled with fury, and the expression of his face was changed against Shadrach, Meshach, and Abednego. He ordered the furnace heated seven times more than it was usually heated. And he ordered some of the mighty men of his army to bind Shadrach, Meshach, and Abednego, and to cast them into the burning fiery furnace. Then these men were bound in their cloaks, their tunics, their hats, and their other garments, and they were thrown into the burning fiery furnace. Because the king's order was urgent and the furnace overheated, the flame of the fire killed those men who took up Shadrach, Meshach, and Abednego. And these three men, Shadrach, Meshach, and Abednego, fell bound into the burning fiery furnace.
>
> Then King Nebuchadnezzar was astonished and rose up in haste. He declared to his counselors, "Did we not cast three men bound into the fire?" They answered and said to the king, "True, O king." He answered and said, "But I see four men unbound, walking in the midst of the fire, and they are not hurt; and the appearance of the fourth is like a son of the gods" (3:19-25).

The king's anger burned as hotly as the furnace itself. He ordered that the furnace be heated seven times hotter than it already was, and then had his strongest soldiers tie up the three men and throw them into the blazing furnace. The blast from the furnace was so intense that it killed the soldiers who threw them in. Yet that incredible heat didn't even faze these three ambassadors of the Most High God!

Nebuchadnezzar stood back at a safe distance and looked into the heart of the furnace. There he saw the three young Hebrew men, bound with ropes, standing in the midst of the white-hot furnace. No, there were not three men in the furnace, but four! And one of them, the king said, was "like a son of the gods."

The core of that furnace was like a cool, pleasant garden to Shadrach, Meshach, and Abednego. They walked through the flames as if through a cooling breeze, praising God. I imagine they might have even leaped and danced among the flames. By the sheer force of his presence, God had turned the king's death decree into a miracle for the ages. It was an event that shook the arrogance of the king.

> Then Nebuchadnezzar came near to the door of the burning fiery furnace; he declared, "Shadrach, Meshach, and Abednego, servants of the Most High God, come out, and come here!" Then Shadrach, Meshach, and Abednego came out from the fire. And the satraps, the prefects, the governors, and the king's counselors gathered together and saw that the fire had not had any power over the bodies of those men. The hair of their heads was not singed, their cloaks were not harmed, and no smell of fire had come upon them. Nebuchadnezzar answered and said, "Blessed be the God of Shadrach, Meshach, and Abednego, who has sent his angel and delivered his servants, who trusted in him, and set aside the king's command, and yielded up their bodies rather than serve and worship any god except their own God. Therefore I make a decree: Any people, nation, or language that speaks anything against the God of

Shadrach, Meshach, and Abednego shall be torn limb from limb, and their houses laid in ruins, for there is no other god who is able to rescue in this way." Then the king promoted Shadrach, Meshach, and Abednego in the province of Babylon (3:26-30).

Notice that King Nebuchadnezzar called them, "Shadrach, Meshach, and Abednego, *servants of the Most High God.*" No longer did he view them as *his* servants, but as *God's* servants. Nebuchadnezzar realized he had no authority over these men. He didn't *command* them to come out of the furnace—he *pleaded* with them! He begged God's servants to come out of the flames, because the sight of them in that furnace had totally unnerved him.

So Shadrach, Meshach, and Abednego strolled out of the furnace, probably grinning from ear to ear. The king had tried to inflict horror and suffering on these young men, but God had transformed horror into joy. Imagining myself in the place of these young men, I would have wanted to say to the king, "We don't want to come out! Why don't you join us in here?"

But Shadrach, Meshach, and Abednego were respectful. They did as the king asked and stepped out of the furnace. All those who had hated them and judged them could see that their bodies were unharmed, not a hair on their heads was singed, and their robes were unscorched. They didn't even smell like smoke!

The presence of God makes all the difference

What is your fiery furnace? What is your impossible situation right now?

Nothing is too hard for the Lord. Nothing takes God by surprise. There is no situation or crisis he can't handle. Not only is God with you in your crisis, but he surrounds you with his presence. He will lead you through the fiery trial with your robes unscorched, without even the whiff of fire about you. He has already planned a way through the furnace for you. He knows the good ending he has waiting for you, and he won't let you down.

Trust God, and he will transform the evil of men into his mighty triumph. That's what happened in the lives of Shadrach, Meshach, and Abednego. When they came out of the furnace, Nebuchadnezzar began to praise Almighty God, saying, "Blessed be the God of Shadrach, Meshach, and Abednego, who has sent his angel and delivered his servants, who trusted in him, and set aside the king's command, and yielded up their bodies rather than serve and worship any god except their own God" (3:28).

Even King Nebuchadnezzar saw that the key to the deliverance of these young men was *trust in God*. And he was so impressed by the trust and faith they displayed that he issued a decree: Anyone who "speaks anything against the God of Shadrach, Meshach, and Abednego shall be torn limb from limb, and their houses laid in ruins, for there is no other god who is able to rescue in this way" (3:29). And then he promoted the three faithful Hebrews to even more powerful positions than they held before.

King Nebuchadnezzar erected a monument to himself on the plain of Dura, and he thought that a ninety-foot pillar in his honor would bring glory to himself and his pagan gods. However, the real monument that day was not a golden statue but a fiery furnace—a death chamber filled with the glory of the Lord. His glory outshone the white-hot glare of the furnace. Today, nothing remains of the image Nebuchadnezzar erected on the plain of Dura. The paltry glory of King Nebuchadnezzar has faded into history.

But the glory of God that shone from that deadly furnace still shines from the pages of Scripture. It is a lasting testament to God's power and presence, and it has inspired faith and hope in God's people for thousands of years. Why do we remember the furnace where Shadrach, Meshach, and Abednego walked among the flames and were not burned? We remember because there was a fourth figure in the furnace, a figure the awestruck king described as having "the appearance…like a son of the gods" (3:25).

The glory that shone from the furnace was the presence of God. Nothing has greater power to change your circumstances than the presence of God. Nothing has greater power to deliver you from evil. Nothing has greater power to turn death into life. Nothing has greater power to weave all the circumstances of your life into good.

The presence of God makes all the difference in every crisis, every situation, and every life.

A simple, practical formula

Sometime ago a woman told me about a conversation she had when she was a child. She was spending the night at her grandmother's house, and her grandmother suggested she read her Bible and pray before going to bed. The girl asked, "How long should I read?"

"Read your Bible until you read something that applies to you," her grandmother said. "When the Bible seems to speak about your life, listen to the voice of God in your spirit and pray."

"How long should I pray?" the girl asked.

"Pray until you weep for your own sins and the souls of other people you love. When you do that, you'll experience the love of God. You'll know how much he loves you, even as you know how much he loves other people. Then praise God."

"How long should I praise God?"

"Praise God until you truly understand that he is bigger than all of your problems," her grandmother said. "When you feel that assurance, you'll have confidence that God's strong arms are holding you. When you have problems, cry out to God until you feel his peace—that's God's Spirit surrounding you, shielding you, and comforting you."

As the woman told me this story, I said, "She said all that to you?"

"Yes, my grandmother told me that she had been taught those

words by *her* grandmother, and she had memorized them as a child. I was so impressed by what she said that I asked her to help me memorize them too." Her eyes glistened and she added, "I have never forgotten what Grandma said. She taught me that night how to know God and experience his presence."

That grandmother had it right. She passed along a simple, practical formula for experiencing God's presence in a life-changing and empowering way. Whenever you put yourself in a position and an attitude to hear the voice of God, to feel the love of God, to experience the forgiveness of God, and to sense the peace and strength of God, you have entered into God's intimate presence.

No matter how urgent the crisis, no matter how fierce the threats, God is with you and for you. His glory shines brightest in the heat of the furnace.

8

You Are God's Agent of Healing and Change

Daniel 4

I once heard about a Christian woman who volunteered to help with a political campaign for her city's mayor. The mayor was so impressed with her work that he hired her as part of his administrative staff.

One day, the mayor came to her and said, "I'm speaking at a luncheon in a couple of weeks. Do you think I should mention my faith when I talk to this group?"

This lady was surprised to hear that he was a man of faith. She had never heard him mention it before. "Tell me about your faith," she said.

He told her he was a deeply committed Christian and had been walking with the Lord since his youth.

"I'm thrilled to hear how much you love the Lord," she said. "The group you're speaking to would love hearing about your faith. You should definitely tell them."

The mayor took her advice, and his talk was well received.

The woman told me, "That one luncheon event seemed to transform him. From then on, he had a new freedom and boldness about sharing his faith. He didn't push his religion down anyone's throat, but he was no longer bashful about it either. He had been afraid that if he were open about his faith, he might alienate voters."

"Is he still the mayor?" I asked.

"No, he's now the lieutenant governor for the whole state. Soon after talking to the church group, he saw his popularity grow in an amazing way. He's become one of the most influential politicians in the region. His political opponents, who aren't Christians, can't figure out why he's so popular. God seems to have his hand on him, and he gets a lot done to help children and the poor."

God wants to use us as catalysts for change, as agents of healing in a broken society. Throughout history—from Old Testament times to New Testament times to the present day—God has used his people to impact and influence society. His chosen instruments are not always leaders of great nations or founders of great movements. But God always manages to place a few of his people in strategic positions where they can influence power brokers and policymakers.

Whenever the world changes for the better, his people are at the forefront of that change.

Daniel's second opportunity

In Daniel 2, we saw how God used Daniel as a catalyst for influencing the life of King Nebuchadnezzar. The Bible tells us that God gifted Daniel with the ability to interpret dreams and visions. And King Nebuchadnezzar, it seems, was a man who was prone to having dreams. Here in Daniel 4, the king dreams again—and once more we see God using Daniel in a strategic way to shape world events. The chapter opens with a message or proclamation that King Nebuchadnezzar sends forth in praise of Daniel's God:

King Nebuchadnezzar to all peoples, nations, and languages,
that dwell in all the earth: Peace be multiplied to you! It has
seemed good to me to show the signs and wonders that
the Most High God has done for me.

How great are his signs,
how mighty his wonders!
His kingdom is an everlasting kingdom,
and his dominion endures from
generation to generation.
(4:1-3)

Can this be true? Is it possible that King Nebuchadnezzar has
actually converted to faith in the God of Israel? It's hard to be sure
about Nebuchadnezzar's heart. After all, he *seemed* to convert to faith
in God after Daniel interpreted his first dream in Daniel 2. But it
didn't take long for Nebuchadnezzar to put up an idol in honor of
himself and demand that everyone in the nation worship the idol. So
King Nebuchadnezzar had a track record of seeming to praise God,
only to fall back into idolatry and self-deification a short time later.

Here in Daniel 4 he again praises the Most High God. And in
the rest of his proclamation, we begin to learn why.

I, Nebuchadnezzar, was at ease in my house and pros-
pering in my palace. I saw a dream that made me afraid. As
I lay in bed the fancies and the visions of my head alarmed
me. So I made a decree that all the wise men of Babylon should be brought before me, that they might make
known to me the interpretation of the dream. Then the
magicians, the enchanters, the Chaldeans, and the astrologers came in, and I told them the dream, but they could
not make known to me its interpretation. At last Daniel came in before me—he who was named Belteshazzar after the name of my god, and in whom is the spirit
of the holy gods—and I told him the dream, saying, "O
Belteshazzar, chief of the magicians, because I know that

the spirit of the holy gods is in you and that no mystery is too difficult for you, tell me the visions of my dream that I saw and their interpretation. The visions of my head as I lay in bed were these: I saw, and behold, a tree in the midst of the earth, and its height was great. The tree grew and became strong, and its top reached to heaven, and it was visible to the end of the whole earth. Its leaves were beautiful and its fruit abundant, and in it was food for all. The beasts of the field found shade under it, and the birds of the heavens lived in its branches, and all flesh was fed from it.

"I saw in the visions of my head as I lay in bed, and behold, a watcher, a holy one, came down from heaven. He proclaimed aloud and said thus: 'Chop down the tree and lop off its branches, strip off its leaves and scatter its fruit. Let the beasts flee from under it and the birds from its branches. But leave the stump of its roots in the earth, bound with a band of iron and bronze, amid the tender grass of the field. Let him be wet with the dew of heaven. Let his portion be with the beasts in the grass of the earth. Let his mind be changed from a man's, and let a beast's mind be given to him; and let seven periods of time pass over him. The sentence is by the decree of the watchers, the decision by the word of the holy ones, to the end that the living may know that the Most High rules the kingdom of men and gives it to whom he will and sets over it the lowliest of men.' This dream I, King Nebuchadnezzar, saw. And you, O Belteshazzar, tell me the interpretation, because all the wise men of my kingdom are not able to make known to me the interpretation, but you are able, for the spirit of the holy gods is in you" (4:4-18).

God, acting through the dreams of King Nebuchadnezzar, gives Daniel a second opportunity to act as a catalyst for truth and change in the Babylonian Empire.

Insight for those who counsel and comfort others

In the second dream, Nebuchadnezzar dreams about a large tree with beautiful leaves. Many birds and creatures find shelter in the tree. Then a voice in the dream comes down from heaven, saying, "Chop down the tree and lop off its branches, strip off its leaves and scatter its fruit" (4:14).

The stump and roots were to be bound with iron and bronze and to stay in the field. The voice then said, "Let him be wet with the dew of heaven. Let his portion be with the beasts in the grass of the earth. Let his mind be changed from a man's, and let a beast's mind be given to him; and let seven periods of time pass over him" (4:15-16).

The details of this dream were perplexing—and terrifying. Nebuchadnezzar called upon all of his wise men, the top magicians, astrologers, and enchanters of the kingdom, to interpret the dream. But they couldn't interpret it. And here it becomes clear that King Nebuchadnezzar, after professing praise for the God of Israel, has now drifted away. Though he is impressed with God's miracles, such as the revelation of the first dream and the miracle of the fiery furnace, King Nebuchadnezzar does not truly place his trust in God. When he has a dream that needs to be interpreted, he goes first to the Chaldeans, the occult magicians and astrologers, the servants of the false gods of Babylon.

Finally, as a last resort, he turns to Daniel and asks God's prophet to interpret the dream. The Bible describes the scenes in Nebuchadnezzar's own words: "At last Daniel came in before me—he who was named Belteshazzar after the name of my god, and in whom is the spirit of the holy gods—and I told him the dream" (4:8).

There is an interesting principle in this story, a principle that is applicable to our lives today. When someone is anxious, afraid, and in need of counseling, we do not need to go to that person and preach or harangue or argue. We simply need to be present and available, willing to serve that person in a quiet and godly manner.

When others see that we are caring and filled with Christlike love, quick to listen and slow to condemn, they will likely ask for our advice. They will initiate conversations with us. It may not happen immediately, but as they begin to trust us, it will happen.

Sometimes people who are anxious and confused will blurt out their deepest problems at the drop of a hat. Other times, they are more reserved and even timid. Be patient. Ask for God's wisdom. Ask him for an opportunity to share his good news. Listen for God's counsel in your heart. Look for open doors that allow you to speak God's grace and truth to that needy heart. And when you see an open door, boldly and lovingly walk through it.

King Nebuchadnezzar says that he called in "the magicians, the enchanters, the Chaldeans, and the astrologers…and I told them the dream, but they could not make known to me its interpretation" (4:7). I wonder about that statement. I wonder if the so-called wise men of Babylon were *unable* to interpret the king's dream—or if they were *afraid* to interpret the dream! The symbols in the dream don't seem heavily disguised or difficult to interpret. They seem blatantly obvious—so obvious that it's hard to believe the Babylonian wise men truly couldn't figure it out. I suspect they knew that if they told King Nebuchadnezzar the truth, they did so at the risk of their lives.

We see this principle in action around us all the time. In the home, at school, at the office, and at church, people often know exactly what they should say, but they are afraid to say it. They are afraid of the consequences if they speak up. So, like the Babylonian wise men, they say nothing. Those who are truly wise know when to speak up, and they have confidence that God will give them the words to speak.

God's catalyst for change and healing

Daniel had complete trust and confidence in his God. His faith emboldened him to speak the truth—but even Daniel felt a moment of hesitation before he could speak the interpretation of the dream.

It wasn't that Daniel was afraid for himself. Rather, he was troubled out of concern for King Nebuchadnezzar himself:

> Then Daniel, whose name was Belteshazzar, was dismayed for a while, and his thoughts alarmed him. The king answered and said, "Belteshazzar, let not the dream or the interpretation alarm you." Belteshazzar answered and said, "My lord, may the dream be for those who hate you and its interpretation for your enemies! The tree you saw, which grew and became strong, so that its top reached to heaven, and it was visible to the end of the whole earth, whose leaves were beautiful and its fruit abundant, and in which was food for all, under which beasts of the field found shade, and in whose branches the birds of the heavens lived—it is you, O king, who have grown and become strong. Your greatness has grown and reaches to heaven, and your dominion to the ends of the earth. And because the king saw a watcher, a holy one, coming down from heaven and saying, 'Chop down the tree and destroy it, but leave the stump of its roots in the earth, bound with a band of iron and bronze, in the tender grass of the field, and let him be wet with the dew of heaven, and let his portion be with the beasts of the field, till seven periods of time pass over him,' this is the interpretation, O king: It is a decree of the Most High, which has come upon my lord the king, that you shall be driven from among men, and your dwelling shall be with the beasts of the field. You shall be made to eat grass like an ox, and you shall be wet with the dew of heaven, and seven periods of time shall pass over you, till you know that the Most High rules the kingdom of men and gives it to whom he will. And as it was commanded to leave the stump of the roots of the tree, your kingdom shall be confirmed for you from the time that you know that Heaven rules" (4:19-26).

Daniel told the king that he, King Nebuchadnezzar, was the tree that had grown great and strong, and its dominion had spread to the ends of the earth. But, Daniel said, the Most High God had decreed that the king should be driven away from among men, and that he should live as a wild animal, eating grass and being drenched with dew. King Nebuchadnezzar would remain in this state until he acknowledged that God is sovereign over human affairs. The kingdom would remain intact—as indicated by the root stump bound with bands of iron and brass, but the king himself would go mad and be robbed of his humanity for a period of time.

Daniel was not like the wise men of Babylon. He saw the truth clearly and spoke boldly. He was God's own man in that hour, uniquely positioned and empowered to stand before the king and call him to repentance. He was God's catalyst for change, his agent of healing. And the healing God offered Nebuchadnezzar through the prophet Daniel was this:

> "Therefore, O king, let my counsel be acceptable to you: break off your sins by practicing righteousness, and your iniquities by showing mercy to the oppressed, that there may perhaps be a lengthening of your prosperity" (4:27).

God, through Daniel, offered King Nebuchadnezzar strong, righteous counsel: Change your ways if you want God to bless your kingdom with prosperity.

There is a lesson for all of us in Daniel's words to the king. When we share the gospel of Jesus Christ and call unbelievers to repentance, we need to be clear and bold, saying, "Renounce your sins. Stop your wickedness. Turn away from doing what is wrong, and begin obeying God."

At the same time, we ought to be patient and wait for people to repent. Daniel called King Nebuchadnezzar to repent, but he didn't force repentance on the king. Obviously no one could make the king do anything against his will. He was the king! And you and I, when we share the gospel with others, cannot force them to repent either. They have free will. If they choose not to repent, you cannot force them to repent. The conviction of sin is the work of the Holy Spirit. The Spirit will work through our words and our actions, but it is his work, not ours. As someone once said, "The gospel is an announcement, not an argument. You share it, you don't shove it."

The core of truth

It appears that King Nebuchadnezzar stubbornly refused God's call to repentance. The Scriptures go on to tell us what happened as a result of the king's refusal:

> All this came upon King Nebuchadnezzar. At the end of twelve months he was walking on the roof of the royal palace of Babylon, and the king answered and said, "Is not this great Babylon, which I have built by my mighty power as a royal residence and for the glory of my majesty?" While the words were still in the king's mouth, there fell a voice from heaven, "O King Nebuchadnezzar, to you it is spoken: The kingdom has departed from you, and you shall be driven from among men, and your dwelling shall be with the beasts of the field. And you shall be made to eat grass like an ox, and seven periods of time shall pass over you, until you know that the Most High rules the kingdom of men and gives it to whom he will." Immediately the word was fulfilled against Nebuchadnezzar. He was driven from among men and ate grass like an ox, and his body was wet with the dew of heaven till his hair grew as long as eagles' feathers, and his nails were like birds' claws (4:28-33).

Notice that as Nebuchadnezzar stood on his palace roof, arrogantly admiring his own power, majesty, and accomplishments—even while his prideful words were still on his lips!—a voice came from heaven announcing that the kingdom had departed from him, and he would be driven away from people to live as a beast of the field.

God confirmed with his own voice the prophecy that Daniel had foretold. The Most High God fulfilled his words to Nebuchadnezzar—and the proud king became a witless creature. But the king was not sentenced to a lifetime of madness. As God had promised, the king's time of madness would be limited in duration. In the closing verses of Daniel 4, King Nebuchadnezzar himself describes what happened next:

> At the end of the days I, Nebuchadnezzar, lifted my eyes to heaven, and my reason returned to me, and I blessed the Most High, and praised and honored him who lives forever,
>> for his dominion is an everlasting dominion,
>>> and his kingdom endures from generation to generation;
>> all the inhabitants of the earth are accounted as nothing,
>>> and he does according to his will among the host of heaven
>>> and among the inhabitants of the earth;
>> and none can stay his hand
>>> or say to him, "What have you done?"
>
> At the same time my reason returned to me, and for the glory of my kingdom, my majesty and splendor returned to me. My counselors and my lords sought me, and I was established in my kingdom, and still more greatness was added to me. Now I, Nebuchadnezzar, praise and extol and honor the King of heaven, for all his works are right and his ways are just; and those who walk in pride he is able to humble (4:34-37).

King Nebuchadnezzar arrived at the core of truth: God is in absolute control of all things. This insight underlies all physical, spiritual, mental, emotional, and societal healing and wholeness: Only when we recognize that God is in absolute control can we be healed. Only when we obey his absolute laws governing his universe, only when we repent of our sin and acknowledge his sovereignty can we truly be whole.

What will you choose?

We like to think that we make the rules for our own lives, but that way leads only to impoverishment and madness. When we follow our own rules, we surrender our kingdom and we descend to the level of the animals. God is merciful and patient with individuals and with our godless society—but only for so long. He will allow godless people to rule with devastating cruelty for a limited time. The sooner we acknowledge God's sovereignty and repent of our sins, the sooner we can be healed and brought to a place of wholeness. This is true both of individuals and nations.

The moment Nebuchadnezzar's sanity was restored to him, he lifted his eyes to heaven, and he blessed the Most High God and sang a hymn of praise to him. When God restored Nebuchadnezzar's sanity to him, he also restored Nebuchadnezzar's honor. The king returned to his throne and became even greater than before, proclaiming, "I, Nebuchadnezzar, praise and extol and honor the King of heaven, for all his works are right and his ways are just; and those who walk in pride he is able to humble" (4:37).

As we study Daniel 4, it becomes clear that this passage presents a choice to you, to me, to everyone. We can choose which of these two figures we wish to use as our role model. We can choose to be like King Nebuchadnezzar—proud, arrogant, self-important, impressed with our own majesty and accomplishments, dismissive of God's law and commandments, unrepentant, prideful, and unbowed. In the end, Nebuchadnezzar learned that those who walk in pride will be humbled by God.

But those who choose to be like Daniel—humble, faithful, surrendered to God's will, faithful to God's commandments—will be used by God in a mighty way. Daniel was an agent of change and healing in Babylonian society and in the life of King Nebuchadnezzar.

What will you choose? The way of King Nebuchadnezzar, the way of madness? Or the way of the prophet Daniel, the way of blessing and wholeness? When God calls you to make a stand for healing and wholeness in a crumbling world, what will your answer be?

9

The Writing on the Wall

Daniel 5

The phrase "handwriting on the wall" has become a famous and well-used idiom suggesting a prophecy of doom or misfortune. The phrase is drawn from the scene in Daniel 5 in which a supernatural hand mysteriously appears and writes a cryptic message on the palace wall during a feast hosted by the king of Babylon.

We should note that, when these events take place, Nebuchadnezzar is no longer king. His reign ended in 562 BC. He was succeeded by several kings who are not mentioned in Daniel's account. First, there was Amel-Marduk, who reigned briefly (from 562 to 560 BC). The third-century Greek-Babylonian historian Berossus records that Amel-Marduk's two-year reign ended when he was murdered by agents of Nergal-sar-ezer (or Neriglissar), his successor and brother-in-law. Nergal-sar-ezer (who was once a high-ranking officer of King Nebuchadnezzar, according to Jeremiah 39:13) was king of Babylon from 560 to 556 BC. He was succeeded by his son Labashi-Marduk, who ruled for only nine months during the year 556 BC before he was murdered in a palace coup. His successor was Nabonidus, who reigned from 556 to 539 BC.

History records that Nabonidus cared more about the Mesopotamian moon-god Sîn than he cared about governing the nation. His devotion to Sîn and his neglect of the chief Babylonian god Marduk caused tension and division in Babylonian society. Nabonidus often spent weeks or months at the moon-god's temple in Harran, where his mother was a priestess. While he was away from the palace, he placed his son Belshazzar in charge of the kingdom

And that is why, as we come to Daniel 5, we find that Nebuchadnezzar has disappeared and in his place is Belshazzar, an arrogant, spoiled drunkard prince. Daniel has lived through the reigns of a series of kings of negligible importance—kings whose tenures were so brief and insignificant that Daniel doesn't bother to list them by name. In this account, Daniel is chiefly concerned with the actions of God, not the actions of kings.

The reliable Word of God

For many years, critics of the Bible scoffed at the account in Daniel 5, claiming that there was no such person as Belshazzar. The historians Xenophon and Herodotus recounted the fall of Babylon when the Persian conqueror Cyrus the Great invaded the capital, but neither historian listed the name of Babylon's king. And Berossus listed Nabonidus, not Belshazzar, as the last king of Babylon. Many Bible critics assumed that Belshazzar was just a figment of Daniel's imagination, a completely made-up name.

Then in 1881, Assyrian archaeologist (with British citizenship) Hormuzd Rassam made an astounding discovery while excavating the royal palace in Babylon. His discovery is now known as the Nabonidus Cylinder, a drum-shaped clay cylinder covered with inscriptions. The original cylinder is now in the Pergamon Museum in Berlin, and a copy is in the British Museum in London. In one of the inscriptions,

King Nabonidus petitions the god Sîn and specifically speaks of "Belshazzar my firstborn son, my own child." This was the first confirmation, apart from the book of Daniel, that Belshazzar actually existed. It is one of thousands of historical confirmations of the accuracy of God's Word.

Critics of the Bible have also challenged Daniel's account because Daniel refers to Nebuchadnezzar as the "father" of Belshazzar (see, for example, Daniel 5:2 and 11). History records, of course, that King Nabonidus, not Nebuchadnezzar, was the immediate male forebear of Belshazzar. But it's important to understand that the Hebrew word for father, *av*, does not only mean "father" but is often used to mean "forefather" or even "predecessor."

Daniel records that, on the day of Belshazzar's feast, a thousand nobles of the Babylonian kingdom gathered in one vast hall. Daniel writes:

> King Belshazzar made a great feast for a thousand of his lords and drank wine in front of the thousand.
>
> Belshazzar, when he tasted the wine, commanded that the vessels of gold and of silver that Nebuchadnezzar his father had taken out of the temple in Jerusalem be brought, that the king and his lords, his wives, and his concubines might drink from them. Then they brought in the golden vessels that had been taken out of the temple, the house of God in Jerusalem, and the king and his lords, his wives, and his concubines drank from them. They drank wine and praised the gods of gold and silver, bronze, iron, wood, and stone (5:1-4).

We need to pay close attention to the details of the story. Belshazzar ordered that a great number of gold and silver goblets be brought out so that his guests might use them. These are the goblets Nebuchadnezzar had taken from the temple in Jerusalem when he conquered the land of Israel. They had once been dedicated to the service and worship of the Most High God. But Belshazzar and his noblemen, along with their wives and concubines, drank wine and toasted their false gods. In their drunken laughter and revelry, they blasphemed and insulted the God of Israel.

The moving hand, the trembling king

Now we reach the turning point of the story. The Scriptures describe for us the shocking thing that happened next:

> Immediately the fingers of a human hand appeared and wrote on the plaster of the wall of the king's palace, opposite the lampstand. And the king saw the hand as it wrote. Then the king's color changed, and his thoughts alarmed him; his limbs gave way, and his knees knocked together. The king called loudly to bring in the enchanters, the Chaldeans, and the astrologers. The king declared to the wise men of Babylon, "Whoever reads this writing, and shows me its interpretation, shall be clothed with purple and have a chain of gold around his neck and shall be the third ruler in the kingdom." Then all the king's wise men came in, but they could not read the writing or make known to the king the interpretation. Then King Belshazzar was greatly alarmed, and his color changed, and his lords were perplexed (5:5-9).

It was the handwriting on the wall! A hand appeared and wrote a message on the plaster wall of the vast banquet hall. Belshazzar watched the hand as it wrote, and his face turned pale. The sight of that hand was so frightening that Belshazzar's bones seemed to melt within him and his knees were knocking. Belshazzar called out to his enchanters and astrologers. He demanded that they interpret the message written by the mysterious hand. Anyone who could interpret the writing, he said, would be clothed in purple, given a gold chain to wear, and be proclaimed the third highest ruler in all the kingdom (that is, next to his father, King Nabonidus, and himself).

Even with these incentives, the king's wise men could not decipher the writing. As the mystery deepened, the king became even more terrified. The noblemen of Babylon were baffled. The story continues:

> The queen, because of the words of the king and his lords, came into the banqueting hall, and the queen declared, "O king, live forever! Let not your thoughts alarm you or your color change. There is a man in your kingdom in whom is the spirit of the holy gods. In the days of your father, light and understanding and wisdom like the wisdom of the gods were found in him, and King Nebuchadnezzar, your father—your father the king—made him chief of the magicians, enchanters, Chaldeans, and astrologers, because an excellent spirit, knowledge, and understanding to interpret dreams, explain riddles, and solve problems were found in this Daniel, whom the king named Belteshazzar. Now let Daniel be called, and he will show the interpretation" (5:10-12).

The handwriting on the wall had caused such a commotion in the banquet hall that the noise reached the ears of the queen. She entered the hall and told Belshazzar, "Don't be afraid. I know someone who can help you." And she told the king about Daniel, who, in the time of Nebuchadnezzar, demonstrated a godlike wisdom. Of course, this pagan woman could not understand that Daniel's wisdom actually came from the Most High God. It was the Creator of the universe himself who gave Daniel the ability to interpret dreams, explain mysteries, and solve seemingly unsolvable problems.

Mene, Mene, Tekel, Parsin

Belshazzar took the queen's advice and summoned Daniel:

> Then Daniel was brought in before the king. The king answered and said to Daniel, "You are that Daniel, one of the exiles of Judah, whom the king my father brought from

Judah. I have heard of you that the spirit of the gods is in you, and that light and understanding and excellent wisdom are found in you. Now the wise men, the enchanters, have been brought in before me to read this writing and make known to me its interpretation, but they could not show the interpretation of the matter. But I have heard that you can give interpretations and solve problems. Now if you can read the writing and make known to me its interpretation, you shall be clothed with purple and have a chain of gold around your neck and shall be the third ruler in the kingdom" (5:13-16).

When Daniel came into the banquet hall, he had no idea why he had been summoned. He didn't have time to prepare a speech. But he had three things that enabled him to be perfectly prepared for any situation: He had a character trait of absolute integrity. He had complete confidence in God. And he had the Word of God hidden within his heart. He listened as Belshazzar described the mystery of the handwriting on the wall. But Daniel was unmoved by Belshazzar's offer of a purple robe, some gold bling, and a big promotion. To a man who was on speaking terms with the Creator of the universe, Belshazzar's offer held little appeal. The Scriptures record Daniel's reply:

Then Daniel answered and said before the king, "Let your gifts be for yourself, and give your rewards to another. Nevertheless, I will read the writing to the king and make known to him the interpretation. O king, the Most High God gave Nebuchadnezzar your father kingship and greatness and glory and majesty. And because of the greatness that he gave him, all peoples, nations, and languages trembled and feared before him. Whom he would, he killed, and whom he would, he kept alive; whom he would, he raised up, and whom he would, he humbled. But when his heart was lifted up and his spirit was hardened so that he dealt proudly, he was brought down from his kingly throne, and his glory was taken from him. He was driven from among the children of mankind, and his mind was made like that of a beast, and his dwelling was with the wild donkeys. He was fed grass like an ox, and his body was wet with the dew of heaven, until he knew that the Most High God rules the kingdom of mankind and sets over it whom he will. And you his son, Belshazzar, have not humbled your heart, though you knew all this, but you have lifted up yourself against the Lord of heaven. And the vessels of his house have been brought in before you, and you and your lords, your wives, and your concubines have drunk wine from them. And you have praised the gods of silver and gold, of bronze, iron, wood, and stone, which do not see or hear or know, but the God in whose hand is your breath, and whose are all your ways, you have not honored.

"Then from his presence the hand was sent, and this writing was inscribed. And this is the writing that was inscribed: MENE, MENE, TEKEL, and PARSIN. This is the interpretation of the matter: MENE, God has numbered the days of your kingdom and brought it to an end; TEKEL, you have been weighed in the balances and found wanting; PERES, your kingdom is divided and given to the Medes and Persians" (5:17-28).

Daniel told Belshazzar that he could keep his gifts for himself and give the rewards to someone else. Daniel made it clear that he did nothing out of a selfish motive. That was Daniel's integrity talking. It's absolutely crucial that when we reach out to others with the Word of God, we have no hidden agenda and no desire for personal gain.

Then Daniel proceeded to interpret the writing on the wall. He reminded Belshazzar that his predecessor, Nebuchadnezzar, had been a powerful but prideful man, and God had deposed him and stripped him of his glory. He reminded Belshazzar that Nebuchadnezzar had eaten grass like the beasts of the field—and came to his senses only when he acknowledged the Most High God as sovereign over the kingdoms of the earth.

The prophet Daniel bluntly told Belshazzar that even though he knew the story of Nebuchadnezzar, he had refused to humble his heart and had actually lifted himself up against God. He had brought in the sacred vessels that had been taken from the temple in Jerusalem, and they had used them to toast false gods and insult the God of heaven.

Lastly, Daniel interpreted the four words that had been written by the mysterious hand: *Mene, Mene, Tekel, Parsin.* The reason Belshazzar and his guests could not understand the words is that they are in the Aramaic language, which is related to Hebrew. The Aramaic language came from Syria and was the everyday language of Israel for hundreds of years, right up to the time of Christ. The words do not form a sentence but are symbolic.

Mene comes from a root word meaning "to count," and is related to the word *mina*, which was a unit of weight and currency in the ancient Middle East. Drawing upon the wisdom of God in order to interpret this God-given symbol, Daniel tells Belshazzar, "God has numbered [counted] the days of your kingdom and brought it to an end."

Tekel is a variant spelling of the word *shekel*, a Hebrew coin; the root word means "to weigh." Daniel interprets the symbol to mean that Belshazzar has been "weighed in the balances and found wanting." Clearly, this means that Belshazzar has been weighed on a moral and spiritual scale, and God has determined that his reign must come to an end.

Parsin appears to be a play on words. When Daniel interprets that word, he alters it slightly and uses the word *Peres*, telling Belshazzar,

"Peres, your kingdom is divided and given to the Medes and Persians." *Peres* comes from a root word that means "to divide," meaning a half *mina*—yet the word also resembles the ancient word for Persia. So Daniel says, "Peres, your kingdom is divided and given to the Medes and Persians."

May none of your words fall to the ground

Daniel didn't mince words. He spoke the truth plainly and bluntly. He called upon Belshazzar to recognize the fundamental error of his ways—his arrogance and blasphemy before God. Belshazzar had used the temple vessels that were consecrated to God to drink toasts to pagan gods. Belshazzar deliberately went out of his way to insult the God of Israel.

Belshazzar's response to Daniel's interpretation is odd, to say the least. Daniel has just pronounced his doom—the conquest of Babylon by the Persians, resulting in Belshazzar's death. The biblical account suggests that Belshazzar takes the news with stoic resignation, knowing his kingdom is doomed and he can do nothing to prevent it. He doesn't ask Daniel, "What can I do? Is it too late for me to repent? What if I change my ways?" Instead, he simply clothes Daniel in purple, places the gold chain around his neck, and names him the third-highest ruler in the kingdom.

That night, the Medes and Persians make their way into the city, conquering the Babylonians and putting an end to both the reign and the life of Belshazzar.

What does God want you to say to the unbelievers around you? What words would he put in your mouth to speak to the scoffers at your school, in your office, or even in your home? How can God use you in the place he has put you?

God wants you to speak the truth of his Word. He wants you to speak words that influence others to build character in their lives and to live out moral behavior. He wants you to speak words that persuade others to trust in Jesus and put their faith in him. He wants you to speak words that honor and glorify him. He wants you to speak words that lift others up, words that affirm the dignity and value of life.

The gospel of Jesus Christ is truly good news. It is positive, optimistic, and life-giving. It's a message that brings hope, healing, and forgiveness to all who believe.

By the same token, when you point people to what is right, you often must show them what is wrong—and where the wrong path leads. Don't be afraid to speak up. Don't be afraid to be that one lone voice, crying in the wilderness, speaking God's absolute truth.

When you speak, God will speak through you. His words will resonate in the hearts of those who need to hear it. Even if they refuse to heed your words of wisdom, God will honor you for speaking his words.

There's another Old Testament prophet whose story is instructive to you and me. His name was Samuel (see 1 Samuel 1–3). When Samuel was a little boy, he became an assistant to Eli, the high priest at the tabernacle or tent of meeting at Shiloh. Samuel slept in the tabernacle, near the ark of God (this was before the temple had been built in Jerusalem).

During the night, God called Samuel, who mistook the voice of the Lord for the voice of Eli. He got up from his bed and went running to Eli, saying, "Here I am." But Eli replied, "I didn't call you. Go back to bed." So Samuel went back to bed. This happened two more times. The third time, Eli realized it was God who was calling young Samuel. Eli told the boy, "Go, lie down, and if he calls you, you shall say, 'Speak, LORD, for your servant hears.'"

When God called again, Samuel said, "Speak, for your servant hears." And God gave young Samuel a prophecy. It was a prophecy of judgment against Eli, because Eli, God's high priest, had allowed his sons to blaspheme and insult God. The next morning, Eli asked

Samuel what God had told him, and Samuel told Eli everything God said, speaking boldly and holding back nothing. So Eli knew that God's judgment was just, and he said, "It is the LORD. Let him do what seems good to him."

And then the biblical account makes a statement that is worthy of extra attention: "And Samuel grew, and the LORD was with him and let none of his words fall to the ground" (1 Samuel 3:19).

What an amazing statement. God was present with Samuel throughout his life. Because of Samuel's faithfulness in speaking God's words, the Lord was with him and he let none of Samuel's words fall to the ground. None of his words were wasted. None of his words were ineffective. None of his words were unimportant.

All of Samuel's words were powerful and beautiful and well-timed. All of his words hit the target. All of his words had impact. None of his words fell to the ground.

God used Daniel and his words in much the same way that he used Samuel's words. Daniel spoke the words God gave him, and he spoke them boldly and fearlessly. May God give you and me his words to speak, plus the courage to speak them without hesitation. May God give us grace so that none of our words ever fall to the ground.

10

Beacons of Light in a
Dark and Evil World

Daniel 6:1-13

If you go to Oxford, England, to the intersection of St. Giles' Street, Magdalen Street, and Beaumont Street, near Balliol College, you will encounter a strikingly beautiful spire-shaped monument, the Martyrs' Memorial. Constructed in 1843, the Martyrs' Memorial houses statues of the three sixteenth-century Oxford martyrs, Hugh Latimer, Nicholas Ridley, and Thomas Cranmer.

A short walk from the Martyrs' Memorial is a cross formed of cobblestones sunk into the pavement of Broad Street. That cross marks the exact site of the execution of the Oxford Martyrs.

In April 1554, commissioners of the papal party, acting under the authority of Queen Mary I (also known as Bloody Mary) held a rigged trial for the purpose of executing these Protestant leaders. Latimer, who was old and feeble, was barely able to speak in his defense. Yet whenever the subject was the authority of God's Word, he summoned the strength to speak boldly in defense of

Scripture and biblical doctrine. Much of the debate during the trial centered on the message of salvation: Are we saved by the rituals of the Roman Catholic Church, or are we saved, as Scripture says, by grace through faith in Jesus Christ?

Latimer, Ridley, and Cranmer insisted that the Scriptures spoke with absolute authority, saying that salvation is through Christ alone. As a result, the panel of commissioners reached their predetermined conclusion (as Queen Mary had ordered) that the three Protestant leaders were guilty of "heresy." They were sentenced to be burned at the stake.

After the sentence was pronounced, Hugh Latimer said, "I thank God most heartily that he hath prolonged my life to this end, that I may in this case glorify God by that kind of death."

For Latimer and Ridley, the sentence was carried out eighteen months later, on October 16, 1555. (Cranmer would be burned at the stake a few months later.) Latimer and Ridley were led outside the city wall to the spot now marked by a cobblestone cross in the road. There they were lashed to wooden stakes and firewood was piled at their feet.

As the queen's men approached with torches to light the bonfire, old Latimer summoned his strength, turned his head to his fellow martyr's ear, and said, "Be of good comfort, Master Ridley, and play the man; we shall this day light such a candle, by God's grace, in England as I trust shall never be put out."

And the news of their execution did, in fact, spread the light of the gospel across England in those days.

Drawn to the light

Whether by life or by death, God wants to use his people as beacons of light in a dark world. In the book of Daniel, we see that Daniel and his three friends, Hananiah, Mishael, and Azariah, were like stars shining out of the spiritual darkness of Babylon. Through the lives of these four dedicated servants of God, we see three valuable principles that illuminate for us what it means to be God's light in a dark world. Each of these brave young men embodied all three of these principles:

1. We are called to reveal the Lord, not ourselves. We aren't called to shine a light on our accomplishments. We are to put all the focus on Jesus. We are to be like the moon, which has no light of its own but merely reflects the light of the sun. We are to reflect the Son of God before the world.

If we were capable of saving ourselves by our own works and efforts, perhaps we would have reason to shine a light on ourselves and our achievements. But we can do nothing to earn a passport to heaven. Our salvation is based solely on believing in what Jesus accomplished on the cross on our behalf. Therefore, we are to live our lives to reveal the Lord, not to glorify ourselves.

2. God does not call us to shine his light in other people's eyes. When you shine a light in another person's eyes, what happens? You temporarily blind that person! God wants us to shine a spotlight on his truth so that others can see and not be blinded.

Christians are often so exuberant and enthusiastic in proclaiming the truth that they do not have any sensitivity toward unbelievers. They don't stop and think about how they come across to unbelievers. Instead of shining a light on the path that leads to God, they shine a blinding and annoying light in the eyes of their listeners.

Some people share the gospel or witness about Christ in a way that is off-putting, irritating, and abrasive. Or they behave foolishly, making the gospel look ridiculous and offensive. Or they are so aggressive in their witnessing that they actually seem to be forcing the gospel on other people. These approaches blind people to the gospel because all the non-Christians can see is the glaringly offensive behavior. They can't see Christ. As a result, Jesus and his gospel are falsely presented.

God has called us to shine the light of Christ with compassion toward those who walk in darkness. Jesus saw unsaved people as sheep without a shepherd, and he was compassionately moved to gently guide those sheep to places where they could be protected and cared for. Shepherds in Bible times didn't use barking dogs or painful whips to force their sheep into the pen. A good shepherd could draw the sheep to him with his voice.

Our gospel should be *attractive* to unbelievers. It should be a fragrance of life in a world of darkness and death. Non-Christians should be *drawn* to Christ by our love, by our generosity, by our willingness to listen and understand what they are going through. We can't force anyone into the kingdom. That's why God calls us to love them into the kingdom, as we are led and guided by his Spirit.

3. *Light does not make a sound.* A beam of light is silent, steady, and serene. When light shines in darkness, it illuminates everything it touches. It enables vision and understanding to take place. That's why Jesus said to his disciples, "let your light shine before others, so that they may see your good works and give glory to your Father who is in heaven" (Matthew 5:16). When our light shines in the darkness, God the Father receives the glory.

People hear what we do more than they hear what we say. We "preach" the gospel much more powerfully and persuasively by our Christlike actions than by any words we speak.

That's the way Daniel and his three friends lived their lives. Their daily walk reflected the light of God's character. They lived with integrity, demonstrated courage, and refused to bow to idols, even when threatened with death by fire. Their faithful, godly service to God shined the light of God's character throughout Babylonian society and impacted the Babylonian Empire in a major way. These four Hebrew men altered the course of history.

And history is still being made in our day. The world is still a dark place where the Christian gospel is increasingly under attack, where the Christian message is largely rejected, where Christians themselves are subjected to persecution and martyrdom. God calls you and me to walk faithfully every day, believing that today just might be the day God created us for. Today just might be the day God uses us mightily to impact history.

History, after all is *his story*. We are actors in God's play. He is using us as his chosen instruments to create this grand narrative that is his eternal plan. So let's make ourselves available to him. Let's live to let our light shine.

The plot against Daniel

As we come to Daniel 6, we see that the life of the prophet Daniel shines brightly, like a beacon in the pagan darkness of Babylon and the Persian Empire. First, his life shines brightly from an open window. Later, we will see his light shine brightly in the darkness of the lions' den.

At the time of this portion of Daniel's story, he is no longer a young man. He has been living in Babylon for more than sixty years. He has served a succession of kings, and now he is a servant of a king known as Darius. (This is probably not the man's name but his title. *Darius* literally means "maintainer.") The Medes and the Persians had worked together to overthrow Belshazzar. Now Darius, a man in his sixties, has been placed in leadership in Babylon, maintaining order in that district of Babylon while the power balance between the Medes and Persians is being sorted out. The Scriptures tell us:

> It pleased Darius to set over the kingdom 120 satraps, to be throughout the whole kingdom; and over them three high officials, of whom Daniel was one, to whom these satraps should give account, so that the king might suffer no loss. Then this Daniel became distinguished above all the other high officials and satraps, because an excellent spirit was in him. And the king planned to set him over

the whole kingdom. Then the high officials and the satraps sought to find a ground for complaint against Daniel with regard to the kingdom, but they could find no ground for complaint or any fault, because he was faithful, and no error or fault was found in him. Then these men said, "We shall not find any ground for complaint against this Daniel unless we find it in connection with the law of his God" (6:1-5)

Darius, the maintainer, has set up a different style of administration over the Babylonian Empire. He established 120 satraps or governors under the administration of three men. One of these three men was Daniel.

Darius could easily see that Daniel was a man of vastly superior intellect and wisdom. He was far more capable than the other two administrators. So Darius planned to put Daniel in charge of the entire kingdom. That, of course, didn't sit well with the various Medo-Persian officials who thought they deserved more of the spoils of victory—and more political power.

There are probably several reasons for the administrators' and governors' bitterness toward Daniel. One reason might be racism; down through history, from Old Testament times to the present day, Satan has stirred up unreasoning hatred against the Jews. Another reason might be the corruption of the officials themselves. Daniel was upright and incorruptible, and he undoubtedly demanded ethical behavior from all of his subordinates. Government bureaucracies tend to be rife with corruption, and an honest leader often frustrates the ambitions of those who would advance themselves through bribery, chicanery, and backstabbing.

So these petty tyrants and bureaucrats sought a way to discredit and depose Daniel. They looked for any grounds, any charge, any complaint against Daniel—but his record was as pure as the wind-driven snow. His integrity was seamless. He had left an amazing track record of wise, honorable service. Few people, after sixty years in public office, could claim such a spotless record. His enemies could not find a single instance of corruption, negligence, or misconduct. The man was squeaky clean!

So his enemies decided that the only way to discredit Daniel was to use his *religion* against him. Their next step was to maneuver Darius into unwittingly setting a trap for Daniel:

> Then these high officials and satraps came by agreement to the king and said to him, "O King Darius, live forever! All the high officials of the kingdom, the prefects and the satraps, the counselors and the governors are agreed that the king should establish an ordinance and enforce an injunction, that whoever makes petition to any god or man for thirty days, except to you, O king, shall be cast into the den of lions. Now, O king, establish the injunction and sign the document, so that it cannot be changed, according to the law of the Medes and the Persians, which cannot be revoked." Therefore King Darius signed the document and injunction (6:6-9).

This sounds so much like today's headlines. The secularists in our society are doing everything they can to drive Christians out of office and out of sight. If unbelievers can't find a *real* charge of wrongdoing against a godly politician, they will claim that the Christian politician is unqualified *because* of his or her faith. They will chant the old canard, "Separation of church and state! Separation of church and state!"—even though that phrase appears nowhere in the Constitution. In fact the First Amendment is intended to protect the church from intrusion by the government, not the government from being influenced by the church.

The secularists have turned the Constitution on its head to make the claim that Christians are constitutionally unqualified to hold office. They accuse Christian leaders of trying to impose their religion on everyone else. Of course, nothing could be further from the truth—but it is a clever strategy (worthy of Satan himself!) for excluding believers from the government, and ensuring that the government is run entirely by unbelievers.

Daniel's enemies examined his religious practices and discovered that, three times a day—morning, noon, and night—Daniel would kneel facing Jerusalem, his childhood home. Jerusalem, of course, was the site of the great temple. As he prayed, Daniel would do two things: First, he would give thanks to God. Second, he would ask God for help. This tells us that Daniel was a man of deep faith with a close relationship with the Lord. Whenever a man or woman of God takes the time, three times a day, to thank God and ask him for help, you know this is a believer who truly seeks the Lord. This is a believer who walks with God, listens to God, and makes choices that lead to godliness.

So Daniel's enemies concocted a clever plot. They convinced King Darius to issue a decree that anyone who prayed to any god or man other than Darius himself during the next thirty days would be thrown into a den of lions. The word *pray* literally means "to make a request."

This idea appealed to the ego of Darius. He liked the idea of being the absolute dictator over Babylon, so the plot of Daniel's enemies played right into Darius's egomaniacal desires. He viewed the decree as akin to a loyalty oath. It seemed reasonable to expect all the citizens of the empire to pledge their loyalty and devotion to Darius. So he allowed the decree to be published, and the ruling was put into effect for the next thirty days.

Darius was a Mede, and the law of the Medes and Persians was that any decree of the ruler was irrevocable—it could not be repealed or revoked even by the ruler himself. Daniel's enemies made sure that Darius was well aware of the irrevocableness of the decree. They did not want Darius to go back on his word.

Daniel's answer to the king's decree

In the next few verses, the Scriptures tell us of Daniel's response to the king's decree—and how this brought Daniel into direct conflict with Darius:

> When Daniel knew that the document had been signed, he went to his house where he had windows in his upper chamber open toward Jerusalem. He got down on his knees three times a day and prayed and gave thanks before his God, as he had done previously. Then these men came by agreement and found Daniel making petition and plea before his God. Then they came near and said before the king, concerning the injunction, "O king! Did you not sign an injunction, that anyone who makes petition to any god or man within thirty days except to you, O king, shall be cast into the den of lions?" The king answered and said, "The thing stands fast, according to the law of the Medes and Persians, which cannot be revoked." Then they answered and said before the king, "Daniel, who is one of the exiles from Judah, pays no attention to you, O king, or the injunction you have signed, but makes his petition three times a day" (6:10-13).

When Daniel learned of the decree of Darius, he went home to his upstairs room where the windows opened toward Jerusalem. And he did exactly what he had done every day since coming to Babylon as an exile: He got on his knees in front of the open window and gave thanks to his God and asked God for help—in direct defiance of the king's decree. Daniel remained steadfast in his faith and in his prayerful walk with God, even at the risk of his own life.

If Daniel hadn't been walking so closely with the Lord, it might have been easy for him to rationalize and say, "Oh, it's only for thirty days. I'll just take a month off from praising God and praying to him and asking for his help. I can resume my daily devotions next month." Or he might have said, "I'll just shut the window. Nobody will know what I'm doing behind closed doors. I'll pray downstairs in the closet. God will still hear me, but I won't get in any trouble with the king."

But Daniel refused to compromise. He refused to change his daily habit of prayer. He continued to seek to be a godly influence in a godless society. He was consistent in doing the right thing.

Daniel consistently did what honored God. He consistently offered praise. He consistently prayed for help. Daniel was consistent in his conspicuous witness. He wanted the world to know that he trusted in the Most High God.

Consistency is a vital quality in our Christian witness. Daniel was a powerful threat to his opponents not only because of his position as a high-ranking official, but because of his reputation for consistent, uncompromising integrity.

Why did Daniel pray in front of an open window that faced Jerusalem? Daniel prayed in the morning, at noon, and in the evening as a challenge to the false religion of Babylon. His prayer life was an open contradiction to the religious life of the Chaldeans, the so-called wise men of Babylon.

The Chaldeans had convinced the people of Babylon that their gods made the sun come up each morning. So the Chaldeans kept the sacrificial fires burning all night to keep this superstition going. When the sun came up, the Chaldeans took credit for it. They maintained their power over Babylonian society by preying on the superstitious fears of the people. Because the Chaldeans sacrificed through the night, they would sleep during the day. They were, in a very real sense, the rulers of darkness.

But Daniel prayed during the daytime. He worshipped the God who governed the affairs of all men. He worshipped the God who had said, "Let there be light," and there was light! Daniel worshipped the God who used the light to create the universe. Daniel was a prophet of the light. He walked in the light of God's law. He absorbed the light of God's wisdom. He reflected the light of God's truth.

What a contrast between Daniel and the Chaldeans! Daniel was a prophet of light; the Chaldeans were rulers of darkness. While the Chaldeans slept, Daniel worked. While the Chaldeans dreamed, Daniel prayed. While the Chaldeans rested, Daniel produced a sixty-year track record of prophetic excellence.

At night, the Chaldeans danced around fires, begging their false gods to allow the sun to come up the next morning—but Daniel slept peacefully, knowing that the Most High God was in charge of all things. The sun and the moon, the stars of the sky, the seasons and the harvest, were all functioning as they should under God's watchful eye. Daniel had a deep assurance, the same assurance the apostle Paul expressed in his letter to the Romans: "For if we live, we live to the Lord, and if we die, we die to the Lord. So then, whether we live or whether we die, we are the Lord's" (Romans 14:8).

Do you have this same assurance? Is God bigger than your enemies? Is God bigger than your circumstances? Is God bigger than the persecution from ungodly people? Is God bigger than all the forces that conspire against you?

The marks of a consistent life

Daniel demonstrated three great hallmarks of the consistent Christian life in his response to the decree of Darius.

1. Consistency means doing the right things every day. Jesus called his followers to live in the day, to be mindful of the moment. He taught them to petition their heavenly Father, "Give us this day our daily bread." That phrase, "our daily bread," doesn't refer merely to physical food. It refers to everything that gives life meaning and fulfillment.

So take a good hard look at your daily planner. Is there a place on your daily schedule for your spiritual life? For your quiet time of prayer and Bible study? What does your schedule tell you about how consistent you are in your walk with God? What does it say about your daily habits as a follower of Jesus Christ?

2. *Consistency means offering praise and seeking God's help again and again throughout each day.* Prayer and praise are not Sunday chores. They should be part of our daily lives, through every waking hour. The apostle Paul wrote, "Rejoice always, pray without ceasing, give thanks in all circumstances; for this is the will of God in Christ Jesus for you" (1 Thessalonians 5:16-18). This means we must direct our minds toward thinking and saying, "I praise you, Lord, for who you are. I thank you, Lord, for all you have provided and all you have promised to provide." This must be our prayer of praise again and again throughout our waking hours.

To pray continually means to be constantly alert to what God desires for us to do and say. We must set our hearts, minds, and spirits on the things of God. The frequency with which we praise him, thank him, and seek his help is a strong indicator of the consistency of our faith.

3. *Consistency means looking to God* first *in all things.* This doesn't mean merely that we should seek God first thing in the morning—though that is an excellent time to praise him and ask for his help. It means we put God first anytime we need to make a decision. It means we go to him first with our joys. It means we go to him first with our sorrows. It means we go to him first with our thanks and praise.

When Daniel heard Darius's decree, he knew he needed to get his mind on God—not the decree, not his political enemies, not the lions in the den, not Darius. He needed to know what God wanted him to do. He needed to remind himself that God was—and would always be—the Supreme and Sovereign Ruler on the throne of his heart.

Spiritual consistency allows us to live a lifetime filled with effective witness and service for God. Daily spiritual disciplines create a foundation on which we can build a faith that will carry us through to our final breath and on into eternity with God. When we become as intimately and continuously connected to God as Daniel was, nothing can shake our faith or break our obedience to him. Even a den of lions holds no terror for those who have spent a lifetime clinging to God.

Daniel's close connection to the heart of God caused his light to shine from that window, illuminating Babylonian society and the halls of Babylonian government. Like Latimer and Ridley, whose martyrdom at the stake shed a light that shone across England, Daniel's life shined a light that still shines from the pages of Scripture. Daniel's faith was the key to his success, his reputation, his inner strength—and his light.

Only one thing can sustain us when the decree goes against us and our enemies plot to destroy us: our daily, intimate relationship with God.

11

The Den of Death

Daniel 6:14-28

The Eighth Amendment to the Constitution of the United States
forbids sentencing convicted criminals to punishment that is
"cruel and unusual." As a society, we reject the notion of subjecting
even our worst criminal offenders to punishment that is degrading
or causes undue suffering. The rulers of the ancient world, by contrast, had no such scruples. Most ancient cultures believed that the
crueler the punishment, the better.

And it's hard to imagine a more cruel and unusual punishment
than the lions' den. As we saw in the previous chapter, Daniel's enemies sought to trap him and kill him. So they maneuvered Darius,
the king of Babylon—a puppet ruler installed by Cyrus the Persian—into issuing a decree requiring everyone in the kingdom to
worship and pray to Darius alone. For a thirty-day period after the
decree was issued, it was illegal to pray to any god or person other
than Darius. The penalty for violating the decree was death—and
the form of death Daniel's enemies suggested to Darius was cruel:

143

"Whoever makes petition to any god or man for thirty days, except to you, O king, shall be cast into the den of lions" (6:7).

I think this cruel and bloodthirsty means of death gives us a clue as to what is at stake here. This is not merely a story of political intrigue, of political conspirators plotting to overthrow a rival. This is a story about *spiritual warfare*. Daniel is battling not just flesh and blood enemies here. He is battling Satan, and Satan is working through Daniel's enemies in an attempt to destroy Daniel.

The apostle Peter describes the kind of cruel threats and opposition Daniel faced in his day, and that we still face in our spiritual battles today: "Be sober-minded; be watchful. Your adversary the devil prowls around like a roaring lion, seeking someone to devour. Resist him, firm in your faith, knowing that the same kinds of suffering are being experienced by your brotherhood throughout the world" (1 Peter 5:8-9).

I strongly suspect that Satan, that roaring lion, worked through the evil imagination of those government officials and came up with the cruelest form of execution they could imagine: being torn to pieces and eaten alive by roaring, hungry lions.

I think Daniel must have known, throughout every day of his exile in that pagan land, that he was engaged in spiritual warfare. He served the God of Abraham, Isaac, and Jacob, yet he was surrounded by pagan worshippers of Babylonian demon-gods and goddesses like Marduk, Sîn, Tiamat, Anu, Ishtar, and Damkina. Every day, he was surrounded by their idols, their loathsome practices and sacrifices, their chants and blasphemies. He was keenly aware of the truth the apostle Paul would later write about in a New Testament letter: "For we do not wrestle against flesh and blood, but against the rulers, against the authorities, against the cosmic powers over this present darkness, against the spiritual forces of evil in the heavenly places" (Ephesians 6:12).

Many Christians today would like to pretend there is no such thing as spiritual warfare and no satanic enemy seeking to destroy our souls. Some people who call themselves Christians don't even believe in the reality of Satan. In other words, they do not even believe their own Bible. But Satan is real, and he is like a roaring lion. I believe Satan inspired Daniel's enemies to select the cruelest death they could imagine.

If you are a Christian, you don't get to choose whether you will go to war. Spiritual warfare is your lot. The only choice you have is whether you will fight this battle with the weapons of the Lord at your disposal. The enemy, the roaring lion, is out to destroy you. How will you defend yourself?

The powerless king

Daniel's enemies have maneuvered King Darius into signing the decree—a decree intended to seal Daniel's fate. And when Daniel hears about the king's decree, he doesn't hide from it. He continues to pray at his open upper window, where he can easily be seen by his enemies. So his enemies go to the king and inform on Daniel, exactly as they had planned: "Daniel, who is one of the exiles from Judah, pays no attention to you, O king, or the injunction you have signed, but makes his petition three times a day" (6:13)

The Scriptures go on to tell us how king Darius responds to this news:

> Then the king, when he heard these words, was much distressed and set his mind to deliver Daniel. And he labored till the sun went down to rescue him. Then these men came by agreement to the king and said to the king, "Know, O king, that it is a law of the Medes and Persians that no injunction or ordinance that the king establishes can be changed" (6:14-15).

Darius was astonished and dismayed when he realized he had been tricked into ordering the death of the prophet Daniel. Despite all of his kingly power, Darius was powerless to save Daniel from this foolish decree—a decree Darius now regretted but could not revoke. Darius knew that Daniel was a faithful servant of the Babylonian nation. There was nothing about his devotion to God that made him any less loyal to the king. In fact, his deep faith and godliness were the very qualities that made him so wise and valuable to the kingdom.

The death sentence was scheduled to be carried out that night. The moment King Darius realized his error, he made every effort, right up until sundown, to save Daniel from the punishment required by the decree. But as Daniel's enemies reminded the king, the decree could not be revoked even by the king himself. So Daniel was condemned to the lions' den by order of the king.

> Then the king commanded, and Daniel was brought and cast into the den of lions. The king declared to Daniel, "May your God, whom you serve continually, deliver you!" And a stone was brought and laid on the mouth of the den, and the king sealed it with his own signet and with the signet of his lords, that nothing might be changed concerning Daniel. Then the king went to his palace and spent the night fasting; no diversions were brought to him, and sleep fled from him (6:16-18).

King Darius went with Daniel and watched as he was lowered into the den of lions. He called out to Daniel, expressing his hope that God would act and rescue Daniel. Then the mouth of the den was covered with a stone, and Darius sealed the stone with the signet of his own authority, plus the combined authority of his noblemen. Then the king returned to his palace where he spent a sleepless night bemoaning the decree he had issued.

The Lion of Judah versus the lions of Babylon

What was the purpose of the lions' den? Why did the Babylonians

employ this particularly cruel and horrifying form of capital punishment?

The lion was a major symbol of power in Babylon. Only the
emperor was allowed to keep lions, and he kept them in pits close
to the palace. The caged lions ate the meat scraps from the king's
table, and their very existence served as a deterrent against the king's
political enemies. To be fed to the lions was a punishment reserved
primarily for traitors and political foes. It was the supreme penalty
for anyone who was so foolish as to challenge the power of the king.

In short, if you dared to challenge the power of the Babylonian
lion (figuratively) and you lost, you would face the jaws of the lions
(literally!). So the lions are symbolic on two levels. They represent
the spiritual power of Satan and the political power of Babylon. But
if we look even closer, we can see an even more subtle symbolism at
work in this story.

Daniel was a Jew, a prophet from the city of Jerusalem, the capital city of Judea. Judea was in the territory given to the small tribe of
Benjamin, though it had been ruled for centuries by leaders from the
larger, neighboring tribe of Judah. Judea was composed of just these
two tribes. And what was the symbol of the tribe of Judah? *The Lion.* In
fact, in Revelation 5:5, Jesus is called "the Lion of the tribe of Judah."

So what we are witnessing here is a showdown between the evil
rulers of Babylon and the prophet Daniel of Judah. It is a battle
between the lions of Babylon—the demon-gods of Babylon and
their worshippers—and the Lion of Judah, Daniel's defender, the
Lord himself. Here again, we see with increasing clarity the reality
of spiritual warfare portrayed in the story of Daniel.

Whenever you take a stand against ungodliness and unrighteous-
ness, you will be subject to spiritual attack from those who do not
worship Jesus as Savior and Lord, those who hate the one true God
and who refuse to acknowledge him as God Almighty. These enemies may come against you and seek to overthrow you, undermine

you, defame you, and destroy your reputation. It may seem that their attack is rooted in a political or social agenda. But in reality, the battle is spiritual. Satan uses wicked people to attack you and, in the process, to attack God and his eternal agenda for the world.

Whenever people plot against you and seek to discourage you and destroy your influence for the gospel, don't be misled. Know who your real enemy is. Understand your enemy's true strategy. Understand what is truly at stake.

Above all, be aware of the enormous power you have through your faith and your obedience. You have access to the power of God the Father, the power of Jesus the Son, and the power of the Holy Spirit. When you stand up for God and you do what is right in his eyes, God stands up for you.

Satan never stops trying to tempt and attack Christians. The Bible tells us he is relentlessly pursuing God's people. He is a prowling, roaring lion, looking for Christians to devour. The prowling lion that is Satan seeks to do battle against the Lion of the tribe of Judah, the Lord Jesus who lives within us through the power of the Holy Spirit.

It's lion versus Lion all over again.

Sealed into the pit of death

When Daniel was thrown into the pit of lions, a stone was placed over the top of the den and sealed with the signet ring of King Darius and the rings of the noblemen of the king's court. The king returned to his palace—and to a sleepless night. He had been tricked. He had condemned an innocent man to death, so he was unable to eat or sleep or enjoy any entertainment. Guilty people frequently suffer intense anxiety.

But what about Daniel? Did he sleep? The Scriptures do not tell us, but the text gives us no indication that Daniel suffered any anxiety whatsoever. I think it's likely that Daniel had an excellent night's sleep. The ungodly king knew the power of the lions, but Daniel trusted in the power of God.

We see this contrast again and again in our world today. Ungodly people are filled with anxiety because they constantly try to manipulate people, manipulate events, and plot destruction and revenge against enemies. They toss and turn all night, scheming ways to gain a little more advantage, and wondering if there's any detail that might trip them up.

Those who trust in God and speak his truth tend to sleep soundly, knowing they have done the right thing. They trust God to take care of the outcome. Daniel undoubtedly slept the sleep of the righteous, even in the lions' den.

The next morning, Darius went to learn the fate of his faithful adviser, Daniel:

> Then, at break of day, the king arose and went in haste to the den of lions. As he came near to the den where Daniel was, he cried out in a tone of anguish. The king declared to Daniel, "O Daniel, servant of the living God, has your God, whom you serve continually, been able to deliver you from the lions?" Then Daniel said to the king, "O king, live forever! My God sent his angel and shut the lions' mouths, and they have not harmed me, because I was found blameless before him; and also before you, O king, I have done no harm." Then the king was exceedingly glad, and commanded that Daniel be taken up out of the den. So Daniel was taken up out of the den, and no kind of harm was found on him, because he had trusted in his God. And the king commanded, and those men who had maliciously accused Daniel were brought and cast into the den of lions—they, their children, and their wives. And before they reached the bottom of the den, the lions overpowered them and broke all their bones in pieces (6:19-24).

The anguished king called out to Daniel—and Daniel answered. He told the king that God had sent his angel to shut the mouths of the lions because God had found Daniel to be innocent in his sight. So the king ordered Daniel to be lifted out of the lions' den. When Daniel emerged into the sunlight, he was found to have no wounds whatsoever, not a single mark from the lions' claws. Why was he unharmed? The Scriptures give us the answer: "because he had trusted in his God."

God's delivering power

In the end, those who had plotted against Daniel ended up suffering the fate they had planned for him. In fact, not only did Daniel's enemies die horribly in the jaws of the lions, but their children and wives were slaughtered along with them. It's horrifying to contemplate, but that was the barbaric "justice" of that time and place.

The Scriptures go on to tell us how God was glorified through Daniel's deliverance:

> Then King Darius wrote to all the peoples, nations, and languages that dwell in all the earth: "Peace be multiplied to you. I make a decree, that in all my royal dominion people are to tremble and fear before the God of Daniel,
>> for he is the living God,
>>> enduring forever;
>> his kingdom shall never be destroyed,
>>> and his dominion shall be to the end.
>> He delivers and rescues;
>>> he works signs and wonders
>>> in heaven and on earth,
>> he who has saved Daniel
>>> from the power of the lions."
> So this Daniel prospered during the reign of Darius and the reign of Cyrus the Persian (6:25-28).

The deliverance of Daniel resulted in greater glory for God. King Darius issued a new irrevocable decree: "I make a decree, that in all my royal dominion people are to tremble and fear before the God of Daniel." This story reveals to us three great truths about the way God works in the lives of his people:

First, *God delivers his people* in *the lions' den, not just* from *the lions' den*. God will not always protect us from dangerous situations, but he is always with us through our trials and crises. We often ask God to keep us out of trouble and controversy, and we tend to think God's deliverance is greater if he totally spares us from our problems. But God never promised us a life free of problems. In fact, the Bible tells us to expect tribulation and persecution—and these trials will come largely *as a direct result* of our witness for him (see Matthew 5:10; John 16:33; 2 Timothy 3:12). If you are living a godly Christian life, you will be persecuted for it.

So we should never expect the Christian life to be a life of ease. Instead, we should expect to spend a night or two in the lions' den. But we can rejoice to know that God will be there with us.

Second, *God rewards those who trust in him as they go through persecution*. If we endure until the persecution has run its course, then God will reward us for our faithfulness during the trial. And if the persecution results in death, he will reward us in eternity. That's his promise. Jesus said:

> "Blessed are those who are persecuted for righteousness' sake, for theirs is the kingdom of heaven.
> "Blessed are you when others revile you and persecute you and utter all kinds of evil against you falsely on my account. Rejoice and be glad, for your reward is great in heaven, for so they persecuted the prophets who were before you" (Matthew 5:10-12).

If you remain true to Christ when you are persecuted, God will reward you in ways that are beyond anything you can imagine. As a result of Daniel's faithfulness, the Scriptures say, "Daniel prospered during the reign of Darius and the reign of Cyrus the Persian" (6:28).

Third, *God has a way of dealing with our enemies that is far more just than any revenge we could devise.* When the story of Daniel in the lions' den is told, people often leave out part of the story—the part in which Daniel's enemies are rounded up at the king's command and sent to the lions' den. Darius wisely understood that Daniel's enemies were the true enemies of the Babylonian state. Daniel himself had been totally faithful to the king; his enemies had manipulated and tricked the king in order to destroy the king's most trusted advisor.

So King Darius sent Daniel's enemies into the den of death. The Scriptures tell us that even before Daniel's enemies had reached the floor of the lions' den, "the lions overpowered them and broke all their bones in pieces" (6:24). Obviously, the lions were extremely vicious—and had been vicious just hours earlier when Daniel was in that den. There is no natural explanation for Daniel's survival; only a supernatural power could have shut the mouths of the lions when Daniel was in the den.

We don't know exactly what awaits those who oppose God and persecute his people. But we do know that God has a plan for those who do evil and reject his love. It's not our job to get even with evildoers. Our job is to do good, to obey God's will, and to take advantage of every opportunity to preach his good news of love, peace, and forgiveness through Jesus Christ. If we are faithful to do good in his name, we can rely on him to deal justly with evildoers.

In the end, Daniel's faithful prayers and habitual praise from the open window of his upstairs room produced a great outpouring of praise to God across the Babylonian Empire. Darius didn't merely *suggest* that people consider worshipping God. He *issued a decree* that people *must* fear and revere the God of Daniel. He made it the law of the land.

As we praise God for who he is—the omnipotent, omniscient, and all-loving Lord of the universe—we begin to understand that God alone rescues and saves, performs signs and wonders, and reigns over a kingdom that has no end. Never underestimate the power of praise and prayer to bring deliverance to your life and your family. Never underestimate the power of praise and prayer to bring revival to a church or a community or a nation. Never underestimate what God wants to do through you and through your praise and your prayers.

12

Futuristic Dreams

Daniel 7

One evening in 1939, the Irwin family was enjoying a quiet evening at home. Mrs. Irwin was tidying up the kitchen after the evening meal while Mr. Irwin listened to the big console radio in the living room, and their nine-year-old son was playing nearby. Finally, Mrs. Irwin checked the clock and said, "Jimmy, it's time to get ready for bed. I'll be up later to tuck you in."

Jimmy went upstairs to his bedroom. A while later, his mother went to check on him, and was surprised to find Jimmy sitting by his bedroom window, staring at the sky. "What are you doing, Jimmy?" she asked.

"Looking at the moon."

"It's time to go to bed now."

The boy reluctantly pulled himself away from the window and climbed into bed. As Mrs. Irwin tucked the covers around his chin, the boy said, "One day, I'm going to walk on the moon."

Mrs. Irwin laughed and wondered at her son's imagination.

Thirty-two years later, in the summer of 1971, astronaut James Irwin stepped out of the Apollo 15 lunar module and became one of only a dozen human beings who have ever walked on the surface of the moon.[5]

James Irwin was a dreamer and a moonwalking astronaut. He was also a spokesman for the gospel. He spoke about how his experiences on the moon impacted his faith in God, and he often said, "Jesus walking on the earth is more important than man walking on the moon." He passed away in 1991, twenty years after his famous lunar excursion.[6]

Young Jimmy Irwin had a vision of going to the moon long before most people dreamed that such a thing was even thinkable. His vision of the future was so powerful that it carried him all the way to the moon and back.

In Daniel 7, we come to another powerful vision. For the first time in this book, Daniel describes a vision that he himself had instead of interpreting someone else's dream. Some of the futuristic events Daniel envisions in the closing chapters of this book have already come to pass. Others await future fulfillment. All are instructive for our lives today.

A dream of four beasts

The dream Daniel describes in chapter 7 actually occurred before the events of chapter 6. Daniel had this dream while Belshazzar was still king. Though Daniel's dream was not a nightmare, he knew it was symbolic and significant—and this dream troubled Daniel's spirit and disturbed his mind. Here is Daniel's description of the dream:

> In the first year of Belshazzar king of Babylon, Daniel saw a dream and visions of his head as he lay in his bed. Then he wrote down the dream and told the sum of the matter. Daniel declared, "I saw in my vision by night, and behold, the four winds of heaven were stirring up the great sea.

And four great beasts came up out of the sea, different from one another. The first was like a lion and had eagles' wings. Then as I looked its wings were plucked off, and it was lifted up from the ground and made to stand on two feet like a man, and the mind of a man was given to it. And behold, another beast, a second one, like a bear. It was raised up on one side. It had three ribs in its mouth between its teeth; and it was told, 'Arise, devour much flesh.' After this I looked, and behold, another, like a leop- ard, with four wings of a bird on its back. And the beast had four heads, and dominion was given to it. After this I saw in the night visions, and behold, a fourth beast, ter- rifying and dreadful and exceedingly strong. It had great iron teeth; it devoured and broke in pieces and stamped what was left with its feet. It was different from all the beasts that were before it, and it had ten horns. I consid- ered the horns, and behold, there came up among them another horn, a little one, before which three of the first horns were plucked up by the roots. And behold, in this horn were eyes like the eyes of a man, and a mouth speak- ing great things" (7:1-8).

It's a dream about four beasts—a lion, a bear, a leopard-like crea- ture with four heads and wings like a bird, and a fourth beast with ten horns. This fourth and final beast is incredibly powerful and capable of destroying the other three beasts. These four beasts sym- bolize four successive empires. Bible scholars largely agree that the lion symbolizes the Babylonian Empire, the bear symbolizes the Medo-Persian Empire of Cyrus the Great, and the leopard-like crea- ture symbolized the Greek Empire of Alexander the Great.

The fourth beast with ten horns is thought to symbolize the com- ing Roman Empire. Daniel described this beast as "terrifying and dreadful and exceedingly strong" with "great iron teeth." The beast devoured and trampled everything in its path. That description clearly fits the Roman Empire. The horns represent later kingdoms that emerge out of the chaos of the fall of the Roman Empire.

The Ancient of Days

At this point, when the fourth beast is on the rampage, something amazing and thrilling occurs:

> "As I looked,
>   thrones were placed,
>   and the Ancient of Days took his seat;
>   his clothing was white as snow,
>   and the hair of his head like pure wool;
>   his throne was fiery flames;
>   its wheels were burning fire.
> A stream of fire issued
>   and came out from before him;
> a thousand thousands served him,
>   and ten thousand times ten thousand stood before him;
> the court sat in judgment,
>   and the books were opened."
>   (7:9-10)

Who is this Ancient of Days? Who is this person whose clothing is white as snow, whose hair is like pure white wool, who sits on a flaming throne while a million angels serve him and a hundred million people stand before him awaiting judgment? Let's read on.

> "I looked then because of the sound of the great words that the horn was speaking. And as I looked, the beast was killed, and its body destroyed and given over to be burned with fire. As for the rest of the beasts, their dominion was taken away, but their lives were prolonged for a season and a time.
> "I saw in the night visions,
>   and behold, with the clouds of heaven

> there came one like a son of man,
> and he came to the Ancient of Days
> and was presented before him.
> And to him was given dominion
> and glory and a kingdom,
> that all peoples, nations, and languages
> should serve him;
> his dominion is an everlasting dominion,
> which shall not pass away,
> and his kingdom one
> that shall not be destroyed."
> (7:11-14)

The great beast is destroyed, the lesser beasts lose their power and dominion, and Someone appears among the clouds and is presented to the Ancient of Days. This Someone has the appearance of "a son of man" (v. 13). This Someone receives dominion, glory, and a kingdom so that all people and nations throughout the earth serve him. His dominion is an everlasting, undying dominion. His kingdom is indestructible.

The Ancient of Days, of course, is God the Father, the eternal Judge—and the one who is like "a son of man" is God the Son, King Jesus. This is a significant and powerful Old Testament prophecy of the Lord Jesus.

The saints of the Most High

Daniel goes on to tell us:

> "As for me, Daniel, my spirit within me was anxious, and the visions of my head alarmed me. I approached one of those who stood there and asked him the truth concerning all this. So he told me and made known to me the interpretation of the things. 'These four great beasts are four kings who shall arise out of the earth. But the saints of

the Most High shall receive the kingdom and possess the kingdom forever, forever and ever'" (7:15-18).

The images of the beasts alarmed and troubled Daniel. He didn't know what to make of that scene. So he asked an angel to tell him the meaning of his dream, and the angel told him that the four great beasts represent four kingdoms that will rule, one after the other, on the earth. But the time of their dominion is limited. And when the reign of the kings and their kingdoms has ended, the angel says, "the saints of the Most High shall receive the kingdom and possess the kingdom forever, forever and ever" (v. 18). This is a thrilling prophecy for all who place their trust in the Lord. The conversation between Daniel and the angel continues:

> "Then I desired to know the truth about the fourth beast, which was different from all the rest, exceedingly terrifying, with its teeth of iron and claws of bronze, and which devoured and broke in pieces and stamped what was left with its feet, and about the ten horns that were on its head, and the other horn that came up and before which three of them fell, the horn that had eyes and a mouth that spoke great things, and that seemed greater than its companions. As I looked, this horn made war with the saints and prevailed over them, until the Ancient of Days came, and judgment was given for the saints of the Most High, and the time came when the saints possessed the kingdom.
> "Thus he said: 'As for the fourth beast,
> there shall be a fourth kingdom on earth,
>   which shall be different from all the kingdoms,
> and it shall devour the whole earth,
>   and trample it down, and break it to pieces.
> As for the ten horns,
> out of this kingdom ten kings shall arise,
>   and another shall arise after them;
> he shall be different from the former ones,

and shall put down three kings.
He shall speak words against the Most High,
    and shall wear out the saints of the Most High,
    and shall think to change the times and the law;
and they shall be given into his hand
    for a time, times, and half a time.
But the court shall sit in judgment,
    and his dominion shall be taken away,
    to be consumed and destroyed to the end.
And the kingdom and the dominion
    and the greatness of the kingdoms under
        the whole heaven
    shall be given to the people of the saints of
        the Most High;
his kingdom shall be an everlasting kingdom,
    and all dominions shall serve and obey him.'"
(7:19-27)

This is not only the good news of the Bible—it is the greatest news of all time! God wins every battle he fights. And that is the key theme that threads its way throughout the book of Daniel. These pagan kings rise up in their pride against God and his people. They attack God's faithful prophets. Yet, even armed with a fiery furnace and a den of lions, they cannot prevail against men of faith, courage, and obedience to God. Those who put their faith in Jesus the Lord not only live forever but live *victoriously* forever. So Daniel concludes:

"Here is the end of the matter. As for me, Daniel, my thoughts greatly alarmed me, and my color changed, but I kept the matter in my heart" (7:28).

This was the definitive statement, as far as Daniel was concerned. The saints of the Most High will one day rule an everlasting kingdom according to the will of God the Father. His eternal agenda will be enacted and his purposes will be accomplished, exactly as Jesus taught us to pray: "Your kingdom come, your will be done, on earth as it is in heaven" (Matthew 6:10).

Three absolute principles

Daniel's dream is a vision of global upheaval, of kingdoms rising and falling, of armies clashing and nations laid waste by the flames of war. In the midst of this dream, Daniel says, "My spirit within me was anxious, and the visions of my head alarmed me" (v. 15). And by the end of the dream, he concludes, "My thoughts greatly alarmed me, and my color changed" (v. 28). These are disturbing images that signify world events that are nothing less than terrifying in scope and destruction.

Yet even such a disturbing panorama of future events did not shake Daniel's confidence that God is in control and his people are destined to triumph. Daniel had lived through times that would try any believer's faith—and God had brought him safely through. Daniel had seen God protect his three friends in the fiery furnace. At the time he experienced this dream, during the reign of Belshazzar, he himself had not yet undergone the trial of the lions' den, yet he knew that God Most High was intimately involved with all the circumstances of his life. So this dream of future events, though intensely disturbing, did not shake his faith.

Daniel had an absolute faith in the God of absolutes. He relied on three absolute truths as the foundation of his life. Let's examine the three enduring truths that formed the cornerstone of Daniel's life of faith:

1. God does not change. World events may change. The global economy could collapse overnight. Our government might tumble into chaos—or metastasize into a totalitarian state. The Christian faith might be outlawed. All our freedoms could be taken away. Nothing in life is certain; everything we rely on is subject to change.

Except God himself! Daniel knew that God alone is immutable.

He is the same yesterday, today, and forever (see Hebrews 13:8). God's character does not change. His nature does not change. That's why, no matter how the world might change, whether tomorrow brings global collapse or complete tyranny, God himself is utterly trustworthy. He says what he means and he does what he says.

There's an old saying, verging on a cliché, but it is true: "I don't know what the future holds, but I know who holds the future." Daniel's disturbing prophecy holds no terrors for those who place their trust in God. Because we trust in God, because our hope is in him and not in our circumstances, we can keep our heads when those all around us are losing theirs. That was the key to Daniel's calm demeanor amid circumstances of uncertainty and upheaval.

2. God's Word does not change. Jesus said, "Heaven and earth will pass away, but my words will not pass away" (Matthew 24:35). We cannot say there are parts of the Bible that don't apply to our lives. As the apostle Paul wrote to Timothy, "All Scripture is breathed out by God and profitable for teaching, for reproof, for correction, and for training in righteousness, that the man of God may be complete, equipped for every good work" (2 Timothy 3:16-17).

There is truth for our lives in every verse of Scripture. People sometimes make a guessing game out of certain Bible passages: What's the shortest verse in the Bible? Oh, it's John 11:35—"Jesus wept." Well, yes, that is the shortest verse in the Bible, just two little words. But read those two words in the context of the death of the Lord's friend Lazarus, and it speaks volumes about the depth of the love of Jesus.

Or take the genealogies of Scripture—the Lord's genealogies in Matthew 1 and Luke 3 or the first nine chapters of 1 Chronicles in the Old Testament. These lists of names (often referred to jokingly as "the begats") do look a little like listings in a telephone book. But even these lists of names are packed with spiritual insights for our lives today. The genealogies of the Bible were given to us to show how God works through the lives of his people to achieve his eternal purposes.

The genealogy of humanity in 1 Chronicles, for example, pauses here and there to give emphasis to God's workings in the lives of certain individuals. Through the genealogies, we see that God's ways are not our ways and that he focuses on the heart, not on a person's rank or power. Again and again, the genealogies disregard kings while spotlighting lowly, humble servants who were faithful to God. Whenever we as Christians feel small, worthless, or unimportant in this world, we should turn to the genealogies of the Bible and rediscover the obedient, humble "little people" who were extremely important to God.

If we ignored the genealogies, we would miss this wonderful Old Testament insight about prayer: "Jabez called upon the God of Israel, saying, 'Oh that you would bless me and enlarge my border, and that your hand might be with me, and that you would keep me from harm so that it might not bring me pain!' And God granted what he asked" (1 Chronicles 4:10). There are four parts to this prayer—a plea for blessing, a plea for an enlarged border (greater influence for God), a plea for God's hand (his comforting, guiding presence), and a plea for protection from harm. We could meditate for months on that one little verse buried in the genealogy of 1 Chronicles.

And did you ever notice that Matthew's genealogy of Jesus contains four women with questionable pasts—Tamar, who seduced Judah (Genesis 38); Rahab, the Canaanite prostitute (Joshua 2); Ruth, a Gentile woman from Moab (Ruth 1–4); and Bathsheba, who committed adultery with King David (2 Samuel 11)? God chose these women to tell us something about his grace and his willingness to use anyone, even people with checkered pasts, as part of his plan to bring forth a Savior, Jesus the Messiah. If he can use these women for such an exalted purpose, he can use you and me as his instruments to carry out his eternal plan.

God's Word doesn't change. Every verse of the Bible is God-breathed so that we may be instructed, encouraged, corrected, and made complete for every good work. Heaven and earth will pass away, but God's Word is absolute and unchanging.

3. Human nature doesn't change—until God himself changes it. Daniel saw a succession of kings ascend to the throne of Babylon: Nebuchadnezzar, Belshazzar, Darius, and a number of short-lived kings whose names weren't even worth mentioning in the book of Daniel. They were all pretty much alike: arrogant, obsessed with power, and often cruel. These kings surrounded themselves with men like themselves: petty bureaucrats and political hacks who were corrupt, unscrupulous, power-hungry, manipulative, and willing to throw their own grandmothers under the chariot to advance their careers.

In all the centuries that have passed since Daniel's day, we have seen advances in technology, increased scientific knowledge, and a steady succession of fads and fashions—but the human heart remains exactly the same. People are the same today as they were in Daniel's day. They are still greedy, lustful, ambitious, dishonest, conniving, and perfectly willing to stab you in the back for a pay raise or promotion.

The most basic and fundamental issue in the human condition is sin. We cannot educate, regulate, or castigate sin out of the human species. It's in our DNA, encoded there since Adam and Eve. There is only one solution to the sin problem: God must transform us and make us completely new. Only God can transform the "old man" into a "new creation" in Jesus Christ (see 2 Corinthians 5:17). Only God, through the power of the Holy Spirit, can enable us to throw off the old self and put on the new (see Ephesians 4:22-24). Only God has the power to reshape us from the image of Adam into the image of Jesus Christ (see Romans 8:29 and Colossians 3:9-11).

We are powerless to change our own nature. But God is powerful to change us, to refashion us into his image and to use us for his glory.

We have just examined the first of several futuristic dreams of the prophet Daniel—dreams that depict horrifying global events. But Daniel's faith in God was not shaken by these alarming images. Take a lesson from this man of faith. Don't let world events shake your confidence in God.

Keep trusting and believing. Keep serving and obeying. Keep witnessing to others and inviting people into God's kingdom of light. Stand firm in your faith and put your trust in the One who holds the future in his hands.

13

How to Pray in Times of Pressure

Daniel 8

S ir Isaac Newton (1642–1727) was one of the most influential scientists who ever lived. He was a mathematician, physicist, astronomer, and philosopher. Most people have heard the legend of how Newton was sitting under a tree when an apple fell on his head and supposedly gave him the idea for his law of universal gravitation. Whether the legend is true or not, his law of gravitation and his three laws of motion formed the basis of classical physics for the next three hundred years.

A lesser known fact about Sir Isaac Newton is that he was a man of deep Christian faith. Newton was as serious about theology as he was about physics. The last book he wrote was called *Observations upon the Prophecies of Daniel and the Apocalypse of St. John*, published in 1733, six years after his death. In that book, he made this observation about Bible prophecy:

The folly of Interpreters has been to foretell times and things by this Prophecy, as if God designed to make them Prophets. By this rashness they have not only exposed themselves, but brought the Prophecy also into contempt. The design of God was much otherwise. He gave this and the Prophecies of the Old Testament, not to gratify men's curiosities by enabling them to foreknow things, but that after they were fulfilled they might be interpreted by the event, and his own Providence, not the Interpreters, be then manifested thereby to the world.[7]

Let me rephrase that in contemporary English: Some people try to impress others by claiming to be able to interpret Daniel's prophecy, telling us what all the symbols mean, how they will be fulfilled, and when these events will take place. Through these rash and foolish interpretations, these self-appointed experts not only make themselves look silly, but they expose the Scriptures to mockery when these interpretations are proved false. God did not give us his prophetic Word merely to gratify our curiosity and puff up our egos with prophetic knowledge. He gave Bible prophecy to us so that, *after those prophecies were fulfilled*, God himself, not the experts, would be glorified.

Newton was not suggesting (nor am I) that we should not attempt to understand Bible prophecy. Newton was one of the most intensely devoted students of Bible prophecy who ever lived. His book on Daniel and Revelation makes fascinating reading. He is simply saying that we should be careful about our motives in studying Bible prophecy. If our motive is to impress others with our knowledge and interpretive insight, then we have misused God's Word. But if we study Bible prophecy, asking God to reveal to us his lessons for our lives, then God will honor our request and disclose to us the wisdom he has for us in the prophetic passages of his Word.

A great deal of Bible prophecy has already been fulfilled. The

Bible predicted that Jesus would come as a baby, be born of a virgin in Bethlehem, preach the good news to the poor, proclaim liberty to prisoners, restore sight to the blind, be wounded for our transgressions, be crucified on a cross, be forsaken by the Father, be made sin for us, be buried and rise again. All of these aspects of the Lord's first coming were prophesied in the Old Testament in startling detail. Then they were fulfilled in the New Testament.

But many more prophecies still await fulfillment. The prophecies of Jesus's second coming far outnumber the prophecies of his first. And many of those prophecies are found here in the book of Daniel.

Daniel's second dream

As we come to Daniel 8, we encounter Daniel's second vision. According to the narrative, it is now the third year of the reign of King Belshazzar. In his vision, Daniel sees himself in Susa, a Persian citadel or fortress located east of Babylon, near the Ulai river or canal. Susa was a royal palace for the rulers of Persia. The Scriptures tell us:

> In the third year of the reign of King Belshazzar a vision appeared to me, Daniel, after that which appeared to me at the first. And I saw in the vision; and when I saw, I was in Susa the citadel, which is in the province of Elam. And I saw in the vision, and I was at the Ulai canal. I raised my eyes and saw, and behold, a ram standing on the bank of the canal. It had two horns, and both horns were high, but one was higher than the other, and the higher one came up last. I saw the ram charging westward and northward and southward. No beast could stand before him, and there was no one who could rescue from his power. He did as he pleased and became great.
>
> As I was considering, behold, a male goat came from the west across the face of the whole earth, without touching

the ground. And the goat had a conspicuous horn between his eyes. He came to the ram with the two horns, which I had seen standing on the bank of the canal, and he ran at him in his powerful wrath. I saw him come close to the ram, and he was enraged against him and struck the ram and broke his two horns. And the ram had no power to stand before him, but he cast him down to the ground and trampled on him. And there was no one who could rescue the ram from his power. Then the goat became exceedingly great, but when he was strong, the great horn was broken, and instead of it there came up four conspicuous horns toward the four winds of heaven.

Out of one of them came a little horn, which grew exceedingly great toward the south, toward the east, and toward the glorious land. It grew great, even to the host of heaven. And some of the host and some of the stars it threw down to the ground and trampled on them. It became great, even as great as the Prince of the host. And the regular burnt offering was taken away from him, and the place of his sanctuary was overthrown. And a host will be given over to it together with the regular burnt offering because of transgression, and it will throw truth to the ground, and it will act and prosper. Then I heard a holy one speaking, and another holy one said to the one who spoke, "For how long is the vision concerning the regular burnt offering, the transgression that makes desolate, and the giving over of the sanctuary and host to be trampled underfoot?" And he said to me, "For 2,300 evenings and mornings. Then the sanctuary shall be restored to its rightful state" (8:1-14).

Here we see a mighty ram standing by the Ulai canal, with two horns, one longer than the other. The beast charges to the west, to the north, and to the south, suggesting a conquering kingdom spreading out in those three directions—and there is no animal, no other kingdom or power, that can stand before the onslaught of the great ram. As will soon become obvious, the two horns represent the kings of Media and Persia, and the ram itself represents the Medo-Persian Empire. Soon after Daniel had this dream, Belshazzar was overthrown as king of Babylon—and the Medes and Persians did indeed conquer the Babylonians as they pushed to the west, to the north, and to the south.

The goat that become "exceedingly great" represents Greece, and the horn represents Alexander the Great. Daniel goes on to reveal the next act of this drama:

> When I, Daniel, had seen the vision, I sought to understand it. And behold, there stood before me one having the appearance of a man. And I heard a man's voice between the banks of the Ulai, and it called, "Gabriel, make this man understand the vision." So he came near where I stood. And when he came, I was frightened and fell on my face. But he said to me, "Understand, O son of man, that the vision is for the time of the end" (8:15-17).

Daniel sees someone standing before him. Significantly, Daniel doesn't simply say, "there stood before me a man," but rather, "there stood before me one having the appearance of a man" (v. 15). Clearly, Daniel believes this person to be more than a mere human being.

A voice calls out from the direction of the river, saying, "Gabriel, make this man understand the vision" (v. 16). This is the first mention in Scripture of the angel Gabriel. He is mentioned here in Daniel 8 and 9 and again in Luke 1, when he appears to the priest Zechariah (the husband of Elizabeth and father of John the Baptist) and to Mary, announcing to her that she will be the mother of Jesus the Savior.

As Gabriel approached Daniel in the dream, the prophet was so overcome by fear that he fell prostrate. But Gabriel told Daniel that he had come to help him understand the vision, which was a prophecy of the end times.

The Old Testament Antichrist and the New Testament Antichrist

Daniel's account continues:

> And when he had spoken to me, I fell into a deep sleep with my face to the ground. But he touched me and made me stand up. He said, "Behold, I will make known to you what shall be at the latter end of the indignation, for it refers to the appointed time of the end. As for the ram that you saw with the two horns, these are the kings of Media and Persia. And the goat is the king of Greece. And the great horn between his eyes is the first king. As for the horn that was broken, in place of which four others arose, four kingdoms shall arise from his nation, but not with his power. And at the latter end of their kingdom, when the transgressors have reached their limit, a king of bold face, one who understands riddles, shall arise. His power shall be great—but not by his own power; and he shall cause fearful destruction and shall succeed in what he does, and destroy mighty men and the people who are the saints. By his cunning he shall make deceit prosper under his hand, and in his own mind he shall become great. Without warning he shall destroy many. And he shall even rise up against the Prince of princes, and he shall be broken— but by no human hand. The vision of the evenings and the mornings that has been told is true, but seal up the vision, for it refers to many days from now" (8:18-26).

Gabriel tells Daniel that the goat symbolizes Greece. The goat, we saw earlier, became "exceedingly great," but at the height of his strength, "the great horn was broken," and "four conspicuous horns" grew in its place. In other words, four great kingdoms emerged from the collapse of the Greek Empire after the death of Alexander the Great in 323 BC. One of those four kingdoms would become the Seleucid Empire, which (at its height) stretched all the way from the Mediterranean coast, across northern Israel, Syria, Babylonia (modern Iraq), Persia (modern Iran), and into Afghanistan and Pakistan. When Gabriel speaks of "a little horn" that grew from among the four horns and became "exceedingly great toward the south, toward the east, and toward the glorious land" (Israel), he is speaking of this Seleucid Empire.

The ruler of the Seleucid Empire was an incredibly evil and bloodthirsty king who called himself Antiochus Epiphanes ("God Manifest"). In 167 BC, he outlawed the Jewish religion in Israel, marched to Jerusalem and slaughtered the Jewish priests, dedicated the temple in Jerusalem to the Greek god Zeus, and set up an idol of Zeus (in the likeness of himself!) on the altar.

Then Antiochus butchered a pig on the altar—a deliberate act of blasphemy intended to insult the Jews and their God. This act became known as the "abomination of desecration" (see Daniel 11:31 and 12:11). Antiochus ordered the Jews, under penalty of death, to worship Zeus, and he made it illegal to keep the Sabbath or even admit to being a Jew. Mothers who circumcised their baby boys were thrown off the city walls with their babies at the breast. It was a time of unspeakable horrors for the Jewish people.

Many evangelical Bible scholars believe that the prophecies that were fulfilled in Old Testament times by Antiochus Epiphanes will be fulfilled again in the end times (and on a global scale) by the Antichrist of the New Testament. See 2 Thessalonians 2 (where Paul calls the Antichrist "the man of lawlessness"), 1 John 2, and Revelation 13 through 17 (where the Antichrist is referred to as "the beast"). In fact, Antiochus Epiphanes is sometimes referred to as the "Antichrist of the Old Testament" because he foreshadows the even greater horrors of the Antichrist during the last days.

The events that are symbolized in Daniel's dreams were *future events*. Daniel experienced these prophetic dreams more than 500 years before the birth of Christ. Alexander the Great lived more than 300 years before Christ, and Antiochus reigned about 170 years before Christ—so the dreams of Daniel depict events that had not yet taken place. Because these predictions were so uncannily accurate, critics of the Bible claim they had to have been written *after* these events took place. But the only reason for supposing that these dreams were fabricated later is the *bias of secular critics* who refuse to believe in the validity of biblical prophecy.

Praying with confidence in anxious times

As Daniel witnessed these visions of the future, he found the experience physically and emotionally draining. He concludes:

> And I, Daniel, was overcome and lay sick for some days. Then I rose and went about the king's business, but I was appalled by the vision and did not understand it (8:27).

A number of parallels exist between Daniel 8 and Daniel 11, and we will return to these symbols and images when we get to Daniel 11. For now, it's enough to know that the predictions in this dream foretell a procession of major events, including the rise and fall of kingdoms, that will take place from the reign of Cyrus of Persia to the brutal attempt by Antiochus Epiphanes to erase the Jewish faith from the face of the earth.

These images appalled and sickened Daniel—literally, physically sickened him. The horrors of those times may come upon us again in our lifetime if we are living in or near the last days. But even if the last days are not coming soon, the days we live in are evil enough. There is great upheaval, violence, instability, and uncertainty in our world. These are anxious times. But we do not need to be paralyzed with fear. We belong to God, and he cares deeply about you and me. So in these times of pressure and fear, we need to go to him and pray for his protection and the peace that passes understanding.

It's a common failing: in times of difficulty or trial, we make prayer our *last* resort, after we have exhausted all other resources in our human wisdom and strength. But God intended that prayer should be our *first* resort whenever we face challenges or uncertainty. When trouble comes, cry out to God immediately. Seek his help instantly. Ask him for wisdom to make the right decision. Then trust God to act on your behalf.

Prayer was always Daniel's first resort. When he heard that a death sentence had been decreed for all the wise men in Babylon because of King Nebuchadnezzar's forgotten dream, he called his friends together for an urgent prayer meeting. When he heard that King Darius had banned all prayers for the next thirty days, he went straight to his upper room and prayed.

Here in Daniel 8, the prophet doesn't specifically tell us that he prayed—but I think we can infer that he did from what takes place. When Daniel was troubled in his spirit by a disturbing dream, what did he do? He says, "I sought to understand it. And behold, there stood before me one having the appearance of a man" (v. 15). How did Daniel seek to understand the dream? I believe he sought to understand it by praying to God for understanding. For at that moment—"behold!"—the angel Gabriel appeared. I believe God sent Gabriel in answer to Daniel's prayer, a prayer he prayed while still in the midst of the dream. Yes, I believe Daniel prayed even while he slept.

So we have to ask ourselves, Why do we hesitate to ask God for his help and wisdom the moment we need it? I suggest three reasons for our strange reluctance to pray:

1. We think we can solve the problem in our own strength.

2. We think we can resolve the riddle with our own intellect.

3. We think we can change a person's opinion or attitude through our own words.

We easily fall into the trap of thinking that God expects us to solve all our problems, devise all our own solutions, and charm others into agreeing with us. But that simply isn't so. God wants us to depend on him, and the way we depend on him is through prayer.

In truth, you and I can't do anything in our own strength. It is God who gives us life, moment by moment and breath by breath. It is God who supplies wisdom and insight. It is God who melts the stubborn hearts of other people so they can hear what we have to say. God never intended that you and I should act independently of him. He wants us to rely on him fully for our strength, wisdom, decision-making, and attitudes.

Daniel clearly understood that God is the source of all strength and all wisdom. That's why he said:

"Blessed be the name of God forever and ever,
    to whom belong wisdom and might.
He changes times and seasons;
    he removes kings and sets up kings;
he gives wisdom to the wise
    and knowledge to those who have understanding;
he reveals deep and hidden things;
    he knows what is in the darkness,
    and the light dwells with him."
(2:20b-22)

God is the source of clear discernment about right and wrong. Ask him for his wisdom in every decision you make. Ask him to accomplish his will through you. Ask him for boldness to speak his message to the people around you. Ask him for success in all your endeavors in his name.

Don't use prayer as a last desperate gambit. Make prayer your first resort.

Three principles for effective prayer

Dallas Theological Seminary was founded in 1924 by Lewis Sperry Chafer. During the school's early days, it was often in dire financial straits. At one point, there was a critical budget shortfall of $10,000. One of the faculty members, renowned Bible teacher Harry Ironside, called the students and faculty together for a prayer meeting. Leading in prayer, Dr. Ironside told God, "Lord, you own the cattle on a thousand hills. Please sell some of those cattle to help us meet this need."

A few days later, a check arrived at the school in the amount of $10,000. It had been sent by a Christian rancher who had no idea that the school had an urgent need in that exact amount. When Dr. Ironside asked the rancher where the money came from, the man replied that it had come from the sale of some of his cattle.

Now that's an answer to prayer!

Let me suggest to you three principles or guidelines to help you pray in times of trouble.

1. Pray with faith. When we pray, it's important that we believe that God can answer our prayers, and that he wants to. When we pray, we need to make sure that what we pray for is in keeping with God's commandments, his plans, and his purpose in our lives and for the human race. If we know that God wants to accomplish something, then we can pray that request boldly, knowing he will do it.

The apostle James put it this way: "But let him ask in faith, with no doubting, for the one who doubts is like a wave of the sea that is driven and tossed by the wind" (James 1:6). God often waits for individual Christians or groups of Christians to invite him into a situation through prayer. Yes, he wants to heal, deliver, save souls, bring about revival, renew hearts, and reconcile relationships—but it's not his way to barge into situations. God wants to be invited. He honors the free will he has given us. Once we invite him into the needs of our lives through prayer, he is free to say yes to our requests.

2. Pray with others. Join with others to pray about individual and collective concerns. Daniel often joined with others to pray; he joined with his three close friends who trusted, as he did, in the Lord Most High. Moses also joined with others to pray; he frequently went into the presence of the Lord with another person, usually Joshua or Aaron. Jesus sometimes withdrew by himself to pray, but more often in the gospels we see him asking his closest disciples, Peter, James, and John, to be with him in prayer during difficult times—especially in the garden of Gethsemane.

Jesus said, "For where two or three are gathered in my name, there am I among them" (Matthew 18:20). So if you are facing a difficult trial or decision, seek out a group of close friends who will support you in prayer, agree with your requests, and add their faith to yours.

3. Pray for God to receive the glory. Pray that the promises and plan of God would be fulfilled so that he would receive all the glory. We sometimes fail to see answers to our prayers because we ask in the wrong way and for the wrong things. We ask for our wants and desires, and even out of the spirit of greed or selfishness. Make sure your prayers are for the good of everyone concerned. Give God credit for the victories he allows you to experience and the goals he allows you to achieve.

A friend once told me he was part of a group who joined together to pray for their community. For example, they gathered together to pray that God would close down a strip joint in a nice residential neighborhood of their city. As they prayed, they also petitioned the city council and they walked a picket line in front of the establishment. They even tried to get an appointment with the owner, but he refused to meet with them. Nothing seemed to work.

The man told me, "We met on three occasions to pray specifically that God would close this business. Frankly, we were getting a little discouraged. We had been careful not to broadcast to others that we were praying, since we were concerned that people would think we were doing this just to take the credit later. At least that's what we told ourselves. I think the truth is we were a little fearful that, after a month of prayer, God wouldn't answer in the way we wanted, and we'd look foolish."

"How long did you pray?" I asked.

"Well, that's the interesting thing. After the third time we prayed, one of the men in the group said, 'I think the Lord is telling me that we should stop praying and start trusting him to act. He wants us to stand in faith, believing that he has heard our prayer and is going to resolve this problem in his timing.' We all agreed with that, so we stopped meeting together to pray about the matter. Occasionally, we'd see one another and say, 'I'm still believing.' But we didn't meet again to pray for God to close that club."

"Then what happened?"

"Exactly one year after our first prayer meeting, the state announced that it was going to widen a freeway through a section of our city. The widening project was going to mean the elimination of a number of businesses to the east and west of the freeway. The strip joint was on the list to go. As a result, the owner announced he had no plans to reopen elsewhere. He was going to retire."

"What a great outcome!" I said.

"Oh, there's one more thing. We've met three times again as a group to pray that every person who worked in that place, including the owner, will get saved. And we are believing!"

Trust God for the outcome

One of the amazing truths about prayer is that, even though you and I often don't even know what we ought to pray for, God invites our prayers, he listens, and he acts on our behalf. So as you pray, look to him for wisdom and guidance even in the matter of *what* you should pray for. Ask him to direct you as to *who* you should pray for; ask him to bring to your mind those who truly need your prayers. Ask for his guidance about *when* and *how* you should speak or act.

You may say, "One of my biggest problems when I pray is that I lack the faith to believe that God hears and answers my prayers." That's all right. Ask him to supply the faith you need to pray boldly and effectively.

And when you pray, praise him for being a God who hears and answers prayers. When the answer comes, thank him for that answer.

You may want to keep a prayer journal. Write down the request you are praying for, and leave space to write down the answer when it comes. Write the date you begin praying for the request and the date you receive your answer. Be open to the thought that God's answer to your prayer may come in a surprising and unexpected form. But expect God to act.

The Lord wants you to take part in his miracles. He wants you to win souls for Jesus. He wants you to succeed in prayer. Look to him for a miraculous, victorious outcome no matter how dire the circumstances, no matter how great the pressure of this moment.

Are you facing a difficult challenge today? Then pray!

14

The Promise—Fulfilled!

Daniel 9

In April 1942, bombardier Jake DeShazer sat in the belly of a B-25 bomber as it lifted from the deck of the aircraft carrier *Hornet*, part of a sixteen-plane formation headed for Tokyo. It was just months after Japan's attack at Pearl Harbor, and the free people of America were delivering their reply.

DeShazer's plane flew across the Pacific, came in low over the Japanese coastline, and clipped the treetops on its way to Tokyo. Right on target, Jake delivered his bombs, destroying a group of oil storage tanks. As the plane flew on toward China, enemy flak punched holes in the bomber's skin. Hours later, the engines sputtered and the fuel tanks ran dry. As previously planned, Jake and his fellow crewmen bailed out of the doomed plane.

Though Jake DeShazer had been raised in a Christian home, he had never received Jesus as his Lord and Savior. Falling through the skies over Japanese-held China, there were no prayers on his lips. He didn't even think about God.

But Jake would later learn that, at the very moment he was bailing out of the plane, his mother in far-off America woke up and felt a great burden for her son. She didn't even know he was flying a mission over Japan, but she felt compelled to pray for him.

DeShazer came down hard in a Chinese graveyard, fracturing several ribs. Before long, Japanese soldiers captured him. They knew he had taken part in the raid on Tokyo, so they took him to a prison camp. There, an official told him in English, "At sunrise tomorrow, I shall personally cut off your head." He spent a sleepless night wondering what it would be like to be beheaded. The next morning, his captors blindfolded him and led him into the prison yard—but instead of executing him, they photographed him.

For the next four years, Jake DeShazer lived in a tiny cell. He left the cell only when his captors took him out for questioning or torture. Sometimes they hung him by his hands for hours or strapped him to a chair and beat him. He contracted dysentery and other illnesses.

Two years into his imprisonment, the Japanese allowed Jake to have a Bible for three weeks. His "reading lamp" was a tiny slit near the top of his cell. He read from Genesis to Revelation, and by the end of those three weeks, he had received Jesus as his Lord and Savior. He had also memorized large passages of God's Word.

One of the first tests of Jake's newfound faith was when a Japanese guard slammed the cell door on his foot. Jake wanted to swear at the sadistic guard—but then he seemed to hear his Lord's voice say, "Love your enemies and pray for those who persecute you" (Matthew 5:44). The next day, Jake blessed the man in his own language and asked him about his family. The guard was amazed that Jake treated him so kindly, and he soon began bringing Jake extra food.

In August 1945, the war ended and Jake DeShazer was released. He returned to the States, got married, and attended seminary. After his graduation, he and his wife Florence moved to Japan as missionaries. They lived among the Japanese people for the next thirty years, leading many to Christ. One of his converts was Mitsuo Fuchida, the Japanese bomber pilot who led the attack against Pearl Harbor on December 7, 1941. Fuchida became an evangelist who preached before huge crowds around the world.

Looking at all the good that came from Jake DeShazer's life after he survived a parachute jump from a stricken B-25, we have to ask ourselves: How many people came to know Christ because Jake DeShazer's mother woke up and prayed for her son?

The murky calendar of Bible prophecy

As we come to Daniel 9 and 10, we see that the prophet lived under persecution and captivity. Though Daniel rose to prominence and power in Babylon, he was never a free man. He never had the opportunity, after his exile, to make a sacrifice to God according to the laws and traditions of his people. He never packed his bags and returned home to Jerusalem. He never celebrated the Jewish feasts and holy days.

Daniel lived in cultural isolation, a stranger in a strange land. Though he was honored and esteemed, he was confined.

For sixty-seven years, Daniel was addressed by the pagan name the Babylonians had given him—Belteshazzar. In Israel, his given name meant "God has judged." But his Babylonian name meant "keeper of the hidden treasure of Bel." After being named for one of the great attributes of the Most High God, Daniel was forced to wear the name of the pagan deity throughout his exile in Babylon.

In that land, he survived numerous political intrigues and death threats. He spent one night in a den of hungry lions. Yet he remained faithful—not only to his God but to his captors. He never neglected his duties. He never showed disrespect to the king. He worked well past a normal retirement age, into his eighties. He rendered faithful service to a succession of kings, even though there was never a hint that one of them might allow him to return home.

Throughout all those years, Daniel maintained his faith and obedience to an unlimited God. He believed in a God who always kept his promises. After living in Babylon for sixty-seven years, Daniel consulted his calendar and began to pray with renewed fervor for the fulfillment of God's promise. The Bible tells us:

> In the first year of Darius the son of Ahasuerus, by descent a Mede, who was made king over the realm of the Chaldeans—in the first year of his reign, I, Daniel, perceived in the books the number of years that, according to the word of the Lord to Jeremiah the prophet, must pass before the end of the desolations of Jerusalem, namely, seventy years.
>
> Then I turned my face to the Lord God, seeking him by prayer and pleas for mercy with fasting and sackcloth and ashes. I prayed to the LORD my God and made confession, saying, "O Lord, the great and awesome God, who keeps covenant and steadfast love with those who love him and keep his commandments, we have sinned and done wrong and acted wickedly and rebelled, turning aside from your commandments and rules. We have not listened to your servants the prophets, who spoke in your name to our kings, our princes, and our fathers, and to all the people of the land. To you, O Lord, belongs righteousness, but to us open shame, as at this day, to the men of Judah, to the inhabitants of Jerusalem, and to all Israel, those who are near and those who are far away, in all the lands to which you have driven them, because of the treachery that they have committed against you. To us, O LORD, belongs open shame, to our kings, to our princes, and to our fathers, because we have sinned against you. To the Lord our God belong mercy and forgiveness, for we have rebelled against him and have not obeyed the voice of the Lord our God by walking in his laws, which he set before us by his servants the prophets. All Israel

has transgressed your law and turned aside, refusing to obey your voice. And the curse and oath that are written in the Law of Moses the servant of God have been poured out upon us, because we have sinned against him. He has confirmed his words, which he spoke against us and against our rulers who ruled us, by bringing upon us a great calamity. For under the whole heaven there has not been done anything like what has been done against Jerusalem. As it is written in the Law of Moses, all this calamity has come upon us; yet we have not entreated the favor of the LORD our God, turning from our iniquities and gaining insight by your truth. Therefore the LORD has kept ready the calamity and has brought it upon us, for the LORD our God is righteous in all the works that he has done, and we have not obeyed his voice. And now, O Lord our God, who brought your people out of the land of Egypt with a mighty hand, and have made a name for yourself, as at this day, we have sinned, we have done wickedly.

"O Lord, according to all your righteous acts, let your anger and your wrath turn away from your city Jerusalem, your holy hill, because for our sins, and for the iniquities of our fathers, Jerusalem and your people have become a byword among all who are around us. Now therefore, O our God, listen to the prayer of your servant and to his pleas for mercy, and for your own sake, O Lord, make your face to shine upon your sanctuary, which is desolate. O my God, incline your ear and hear. Open your eyes and see our desolations, and the city that is called by your name. For we do not present our pleas before you because of our righteousness, but because of your great mercy. O Lord, hear; O Lord, forgive. O Lord, pay attention and act. Delay not, for your own sake, O my God, because your city and your people are called by your name" (9:1-19).

Daniel has carefully studied Jeremiah's prophecy, he has counted up his own years in the royal court of Babylon, and he has witnessed the fall of Babylon to the invading Medes and Persians under Darius. He knows that the end of the seventy-year period mentioned in Jeremiah's prophecy is almost complete. The deliverance of the Jewish exiles draws near. We can draw some important lessons for our own spiritual walk from Daniel's prayer.

1. Study God's Word and apply it to your own life. Bible study was no mere intellectual exercise for Daniel. He put his heart and soul into understanding what God was saying through his Word.

Daniel refers to Jeremiah 25:12, in which Jeremiah prophesied that the captivity in Babylon would last for seventy years. In Jeremiah chapters 25 through 30, the prophet predicted that Jerusalem would be laid waste, that the Jewish people would be carried off into Babylon and would serve Nebuchadnezzar. But he also predicted that, after seventy years of exile, the Lord would restore his people to the lands of Israel and Judah and the city of Jerusalem. At the end of that time, Babylon would be destroyed and made desolate forever. The Lord said:

> "I will bring upon that land all the words that I have
> uttered against it, everything written in this book, which
> Jeremiah prophesied against all the nations. For many
> nations and great kings shall make slaves even of them,
> and I will recompense them according to their deeds and
> the work of their hands" (Jeremiah 25:13-14).

Daniel had been exiled for sixty-seven years—and he could do the math. He knew the fulfillment of Jeremiah's prophecy might be close at hand.

2. Give God room to act according to his timetable. Daniel knew there was nothing in the prophecies of Jeremiah that specifically promised that, on the stroke of the beginning of the seventieth year of captivity, the Jewish people would be allowed to leave Babylon and return in caravans to Jerusalem. Daniel knew the promise of God, but he didn't know the precise timing or method by which God would keep his promise.

This is a critically important principle for you and me to remember as we face persecution and troubled times. We know that God will prevail in carrying out the promises in his Word. But just *when* and *how* he chooses to fulfill his promises are questions we cannot answer.

3. Pray with praise and confession. Once Daniel understood what God was saying to him through the prophet Jeremiah, he immediately lifted his face toward heaven, sought the Lord through prayer and fasting, sackcloth and ashes, and prayed, beginning by praising "the great and awesome God" and confessing the sin of his people. "We have sinned and done wrong and acted wickedly and rebelled," he prayed, "turning aside from your commandments and rules...To you, O Lord, belongs righteousness, but to us open shame" (9:4-5,7).

It is a sign of spiritual maturity when we open our prayers with praise and confession to God. Praise and confession signify that we acknowledge God's immensity and our unworthiness.

4. Pray with a humble, contrite heart. Daniel identified with his people as he prayed. His confession to God is not "*they* have sinned," but "*we* have sinned." Daniel was one of the most faithful and obedient Hebrews alive on the planet, yet he included himself in his confession and petition for the Jewish people. That's the essence of prayerful humility—and God loves a humble and contrite heart.

5. Pour out your emotions in prayer. Daniel held nothing back. He prayed with deep emotion and intensity before the Lord. We can see Daniel's churning emotions in verses 18 and 19, where he prays, "O my God, incline your ear and hear. Open your eyes and see our desolations, and the city that is called by your name. For we do not present our pleas before you because of our righteousness, but because of your great mercy. O Lord, hear; O Lord, forgive. O

Lord, pay attention and act. Delay not, for your own sake, O my God, because your city and your people are called by your name."

Daniel and his people have suffered greatly—but, Daniel says, their suffering is not unjust. The people deserve their suffering. Daniel does not ask God for justice but for mercy. He asks God to act without delay on behalf of his wayward but contrite people. He pleads with God to end the desolation of Jerusalem.

The return of the angel Gabriel

Even before Daniel has finished praying, God again sends the angel Gabriel to him with an answer:

> While I was speaking and praying, confessing my sin and the sin of my people Israel, and presenting my plea before the LORD my God for the holy hill of my God, while I was speaking in prayer, the man Gabriel, whom I had seen in the vision at the first, came to me in swift flight at the time of the evening sacrifice. He made me understand, speaking with me and saying, "O Daniel, I have now come out to give you insight and understanding. At the beginning of your pleas for mercy a word went out, and I have come to tell it to you, for you are greatly loved. Therefore consider the word and understand the vision.
>
> "Seventy weeks are decreed about your people and your holy city, to finish the transgression, to put an end to sin, and to atone for iniquity, to bring in everlasting righteousness, to seal both vision and prophet, and to anoint a most holy place. Know therefore and understand that from the going out of the word to restore and build Jerusalem to the coming of an anointed one, a prince, there shall be seven weeks. Then for sixty-two weeks it shall be built again with squares and moat, but in a troubled time. And after the sixty-two weeks, an anointed one shall be cut off and shall have nothing. And the people of the prince who

is to come shall destroy the city and the sanctuary. Its end shall come with a flood, and to the end there shall be war. Desolations are decreed. And he shall make a strong covenant with many for one week, and for half of the week he shall put an end to sacrifice and offering. And on the wing of abominations shall come one who makes desolate, until the decreed end is poured out on the desolator" (9:20-27).

God's dramatic answer comes while Daniel is still in prayer. Sometimes God seems to delay in answering our prayers—and sometimes he answers even before we have finished praying!

Daniel draws our attention to a significant detail when he writes that the angel Gabriel "came to me in swift flight at the time of the evening sacrifice." Why is this moment significant? It's significant because the time of the evening sacrifice was when Moses offered the Passover lamb in Exodus 12:6, and it is the moment when Jesus was crucified, as recorded in Matthew 27:45. The message Gabriel brings is a prophecy of the coming Messiah—the Lamb of God, our Passover sacrifice, who takes away the sin of the world. It's appropriate that this message should come to Daniel at the time of the evening sacrifice.

In this passage, Gabriel reveals to Daniel the prophecy of the seventy weeks. Bible scholars are nearly unanimous in their agreement that this prophecy refers to seventy sets of seven years. Gabriel tells Daniel that a series of amazing events will take place during this period of time. As we look back in history, we make an amazing discovery: the events Gabriel foretold have occurred right on schedule and in exacting detail.

The messianic timetable in Daniel 9

Sir Isaac Newton makes an amazing statement: "To reject [Daniel's] Prophecies is to reject the Christian religion. For this religion is founded upon his Prophecy concerning the Messiah."[8]

I believe we see the confirmation of Newton's claim as we examine the life of Jesus and discover how the Lord's public ministry appears to be governed by the timetable of the prophecy in Daniel 9. For example, in the account of the Lord's first miracle at the wedding in Cana (John 2:1-11), we see that the bridegroom has run out of wine. So Mary, the mother of Jesus, approaches him and urges him to perform a spectacular miracle. Jesus replies, "Woman, what does this have to do with me? My hour has not yet come" (v. 4). Then quietly, without sensation or fanfare, Jesus performs his first miracle, transforming water into wine. The only ones who are in the know about this miracle are his disciples and a few servants. Jesus refuses to announce himself as the promised Messiah because *his time has not yet come*.

Later, some of the Lord's family members tell him, "Leave here and go to Judea, that your disciples also may see the works you are doing. For no one works in secret if he seeks to be known openly. If you do these things, show yourself to the world." But Jesus refuses, saying, "My time has not yet come" (see John 7:1-7). Once again, Jesus refuses to announce himself as the Messiah because *his time has not yet come*.

Again and again, Jesus refers to a secret timetable for his ministry. Once, while walking with his disciples to the town of Caesarea Philippi, he asks them, "Who do people say that the Son of Man is?" In the course of this conversation, Peter makes his wonderful confession, "You are the Christ [that is, the Messiah], the Son of the living God." Jesus blesses and affirms Peter because God has revealed this truth to him—then he adds that the disciples should tell no one who he really is (see Matthew 16:13-20). Why keep his identity a secret? Because *his time has not yet come*.

Finally, after three years of teaching and healing, Jesus approaches the end of his earthly ministry. On the Sunday before his crucifixion, he comes into Jerusalem riding on a donkey. Throngs of people spread palm branches across his path, shouting, "Blessed is the King who comes in the name of the Lord! Peace in heaven and glory in the highest!" The Lord's enemies shout to him, saying, "Teacher, rebuke your disciples!" But Jesus replies, "I tell you, if these were silent, the very stones would cry out" (see Luke 19:37-40).

Again and again, Jesus has kept his identity a secret, saying, "My time has not yet come." But on the day we know as Palm Sunday, Jesus permits the people to announce him and receive him as the promised Messiah. Why? Because Jesus knew that his time had finally come. The timetable was fulfilled.

And how did Jesus know this? He knew it because of the precise timetable Gabriel gave to Daniel in Daniel 9.

Jesus had once told the religious leaders who opposed him, "You search the Scriptures because you think that in them you have eternal life; and it is they that bear witness about me" (John 5:39). In other words, Jesus told the religious leaders that all the Old Testament prophecies pointed to Jesus as the focal point of history.

The most startling and eerily precise of all the Old Testament prophecies of the Messiah is found in Daniel 9:25: "Know therefore and understand that from the going out of the word to restore and build Jerusalem to the coming of an anointed one, a prince, there shall be seven weeks. Then for sixty-two weeks it shall be built again with squares and moat, but in a troubled time."

Gabriel spoke these words to Daniel while the Jewish people were still in exile in Babylon, and centuries before the birth of Christ. Yet these words set forth a precise timetable predicting when the Messiah—"an anointed one, a prince"—would be presented before all the people. The decree to rebuild Jerusalem would be issued, then there would be seven "weeks" (or seven "sevens" of years) plus sixty-two "weeks" (sixty-two "sevens" of years), at which time the Messiah, the anointed one, would appear.

Frederick A. Larson is a scholar, philosopher, and attorney who studied under the late Francis Schaeffer at the famed Christian leadership community L'Abri in Switzerland. Larson made a careful investigation of the Daniel 9 prophecy and came to a number of startling conclusions. He began with the assumption that the "weeks" are seven-year periods. With that assumption as a starting point, the math is simple: 7 times 7 equals 49, and 62 times 7 equals 434. Add 49 plus 434 and you get 483. So if Daniel's prophecy is correct, the Messiah ("anointed one") would be presented to Israel 483 years after the decree to rebuild Jerusalem.

Problem: If you use modern 365-day years as your measurement, you will arrive at the wrong answer. In Daniel's day, the world measured years according to a 360-day calendar. Mathematician Sir James Jeans explained in *The Growth of Physical Science* (1947), "When the early Babylonians first tried to measure the number of days in the year, they would find it was about 360. More than 2000 years before Christ they agreed to call it 360 as an approximation, dividing their year into 12 months of 30 days each, and inserting extra months now and then as needed."[9]

Frederick Larson knew that 483 ancient-style years of 360 days would equal 476 years on our calendar. When was the decree to rebuild Jerusalem issued? According to Larson, "The prophet Nehemiah records such a decree, and he dates it as the twentieth year of Artaxerxes. On our calendar, that date is 444 BC." Counting 476 years after 444 BC (and we have to remember that there was no "year zero") we find that the date that Gabriel gave for the coming of the Messiah would be AD 33.

Larson fine-tunes his calculations by reminding us that, before Jesus was crucified, he celebrated the Passover in the upper room with his disciples. Passover begins on the fourteenth day of the Jewish month of Nisan. Jesus made his triumphant entry into Jerusalem on Palm Sunday, and he was crucified the following Friday, the day of preparation before Saturday, the Sabbath day. Clearly, the crucifixion must have occurred in a year when the fourteenth of Nisan fell on a Friday. The Jews measured a day from twilight to twilight, so the Jewish Friday actually began on our Thursday night.

Jesus was condemned to death by Pontius Pilate, who was the Roman procurator of Judea from AD 26 through 36. The fourteenth of Nisan fell on a Friday only twice during those years—on April 7, AD 30 and April 3, AD 33. Combine this data with Gabriel's prophecy in Daniel 9, and it is clear that Jesus must have been crucified on Friday, April 3, AD 33. Therefore, the Lord's triumphal entry into Jerusalem on the first Palm Sunday occurred on Sunday, March 29, AD 33.

Jesus knew exactly when his time would come, and he kept his date with divinely appointed destiny. Bible scholars estimate there are at least three hundred prophecies that point to the coming of the Messiah. Scattered across the Old Testament, from Genesis to Malachi, those prophecies predict his birth, ministry, death, and resurrection. As Jesus told his opponents, those prophecies point directly to him.

If the Old Testament pointed so clearly to Jesus, and even gave us the timetable of his appearance, why didn't the people see his timetable and honor him as their king? The answer is simple: Prophecies are easier to understand with hindsight than with foresight. Remember the words of Sir Isaac Newton, who told us that God gave the Old Testament prophecies "not to gratify men's curiosities by enabling them to foreknow things, but that after they were fulfilled they might be interpreted by the event."

The Pharisees and Sadducees didn't know when the Lord's time would come. Mary, the mother of Jesus, didn't know when his time would come. His family members didn't know when his time would come. His disciples didn't know when his time would come. But Jesus knew. He had studied the Scriptures and he knew exactly when the Messiah, the anointed one, was scheduled to appear.

Today, with the benefit of hindsight, and the benefit of Daniel 9, we also know. And seeing God's Old Testament promises fulfilled in the New Testament inspires our faith and our faithfulness to Jesus, the promised Messiah.

15

The Invisible War

Daniel 10–11

I once watched a blind man who demonstrated the most incredible skills as a public speaker. He could walk all around the stage as he spoke, and he could even step right up to the edge of the platform, so that if he took one more step he'd tumble into the orchestra pit. Yet he never stumbled, never lost track of where he was, never had a misstep. When he spoke to the audience, he would look out and actually make eye contact with individuals who asked him questions even though he was unable to see them. How did he do it?

The answer sounds simple, but it involves a skill he acquired after years of intense practice. He would go out on the stage before the event, walk all around it, counting the steps from point A to point B to point C, and he would map the stage in his mind. He would memorize it until he could actually "see" the stage in his imagination. Through years of practice, he had learned how to locate voices so that when people spoke to him, he could meet them eye to eye, even though he was blind.

Through experience, practice, and focus, this man learned to walk and talk by "faith" in his mental image of his surroundings. He was a living example of Paul's words, "For we walk by faith, not by sight" (2 Corinthians 5:7). Ironically, this man's faith was not a "blind faith." It was an *informed* faith. It was a *tested* faith. It was a *proven* faith.

This blind man had faith that he could go out on the stage he had carefully mapped in his mind, and he could perform as effectively as if he had twenty-twenty vision. He had faith that no one had gone up on the stage when he was not aware of it and placed a chair or a roller skate or a banana peel where he would be walking. He had faith that he could remember the exact number of steps from one place to another. His faith enabled him to do the seemingly impossible.

You and I can experience the same kind of faith—not a blind faith, but an informed, tested, proven faith. We can experience daily the strength and guidance and power of God. We can immerse our minds in the truth of God's Word. We can test out this faith moment by moment, day by day, and see for ourselves that God can be trusted. He is our Provider, our Protector, our Problem-Solver—if we step out in faith, believing he will be there to hold our hand and guide us through the darkness and into his light.

As we come to the concluding chapters of the book of Daniel, this faithful prophet again experiences a terrifying vision. He sees images that are disturbing and hard to understand. His mind is troubled with questions, and the answers are not quick in coming. There is darkness ahead for Daniel—the darkness of terrifying visions.

But God knows that his servant Daniel is strong enough and bold enough to shoulder the weight of these visions. And in the next few pages, this faithful prophet will pull back the curtain of the future and reveal his visions to you and me.

This present darkness

Daniel chapters 10 through 12 contain a single long vision that Daniel experienced during the third year of the Persian emperor Cyrus. Daniel would have witnessed this vision in 533 BC. The opening verses of the Old Testament book of Ezra tell us that Cyrus set the Hebrew people free to return to their homeland. A clay cylinder document, the Cyrus Cylinder (excavated from the ruins of Babylon in 1879), agrees with the biblical accounts. Cyrus records on the cylinder, "I gathered all their inhabitants and returned to them their dwellings."[10] Because Cyrus ended Israel's humiliating exile in Babylon, this Persian emperor holds an honored place in Judaism.

Daniel experienced this last prophetic dream after the Jews had begun their return to their homeland. This vision contains fascinating insights into the nature of spiritual reality. Here we catch a glimpse behind the scenes of our world, and we sense there are forces and rulers of the unseen world, and these hidden spirits are pulling the levers and flipping the switches that operate the unseen machinery of human reality. As the apostle Paul reminds us, "For we do not wrestle against flesh and blood, but against the rulers, against the authorities, against the cosmic powers over this present darkness, against the spiritual forces of evil in the heavenly places" (Ephesians 6:12).

Daniel opens the section with these words:

> In the third year of Cyrus king of Persia a word was revealed to Daniel, who was named Belteshazzar. And the word was true, and it was a great conflict. And he understood the word and had understanding of the vision (10:1).

Daniel tells us he has received a word, a message, about a great conflict—a spiritual conflict. It is the same war Paul writes about, a war against "this present darkness." It's not a struggle between flesh-and-blood combatants, but between invisible but very real spiritual forces. Daniel continues:

In those days I, Daniel, was mourning for three weeks. I ate no delicacies, no meat or wine entered my mouth, nor did I anoint myself at all, for the full three weeks. On the twenty-fourth day of the first month, as I was standing on the bank of the great river (that is, the Tigris) I lifted up my eyes and looked, and behold, a man clothed in linen, with a belt of fine gold from Uphaz around his waist. His body was like beryl, his face like the appearance of lightning, his eyes like flaming torches, his arms and legs like the gleam of burnished bronze, and the sound of his words like the sound of a multitude. And I, Daniel, alone saw the vision, for the men who were with me did not see the vision, but a great trembling fell upon them, and they fled to hide themselves. So I was left alone and saw this great vision, and no strength was left in me. My radiant appearance was fearfully changed, and I retained no strength. Then I heard the sound of his words, and as I heard the sound of his words, I fell on my face in deep sleep with my face to the ground.

And behold, a hand touched me and set me trembling on my hands and knees. And he said to me, "O Daniel, man greatly loved, understand the words that I speak to you, and stand upright, for now I have been sent to you." And when he had spoken this word to me, I stood up trembling. Then he said to me, "Fear not, Daniel, for from the first day that you set your heart to understand and humbled yourself before your God, your words have been heard, and I have come because of your words. The prince of the kingdom of Persia withstood me twenty-one days, but Michael, one of the chief princes, came to help me, for I was left there with the kings of Persia, and came to make you understand what is to happen to your people in the latter days. For the vision is for days yet to come."

When he had spoken to me according to these words, I turned my face toward the ground and was mute. And behold, one in the likeness of the children of man touched my lips. Then I opened my mouth and spoke. I said to him who stood before me, "O my lord, by reason of the vision pains have come upon me, and I retain no strength. How can my lord's servant talk with my lord? For now no strength remains in me, and no breath is left in me."

Again one having the appearance of a man touched me and strengthened me. And he said, "O man greatly loved, fear not, peace be with you; be strong and of good courage." And as he spoke to me, I was strengthened and said, "Let my lord speak, for you have strengthened me." Then he said, "Do you know why I have come to you? But now I will return to fight against the prince of Persia; and when I go out, behold, the prince of Greece will come. But I will tell you what is inscribed in the book of truth: there is none who contends by my side against these except Michael, your prince" (10:2-21).

These verses spotlight the invisible forces that move events in the visible world. If you have ever wondered why evil seems to reign in the affairs of nations, including our own nation, here's the reason: unseen rulers war against God, and these rulers use individuals and nations as their proxy agents to carry on this hidden struggle.

As Daniel 10 opens, Daniel stands beside the Tigris River. Other people are around him, and we don't know if those people are actually with Daniel or they just happened to be there at the same time. Daniel has been fasting and praying for three weeks. Suddenly, he sees a man dressed in white linen, with a belt of gold around his waist; the man's face shines like lightning and his eyes burn like fire. His voice sounds like a multitude of voices all speaking at once. Who is this man?

Perhaps we gain a clue from a New Testament book of prophecy. In Revelation 1:13-16, the apostle John has a vision of Jesus Christ appearing to him dressed in a robe bound with a golden belt, with hair as white as wool, a face that shines like the sun, and eyes like blazing fire. His voice sounds like the sound of rushing water.

There are common features to both Daniel's vision and John's vision. In each case, these men are given a glimpse behind the curtain of reality. They are permitted to see this invisible, spiritual battle now being waged by the forces and rulers of spiritual darkness. Throughout the Old Testament there are other instances where a mysterious man appears to one of God's saints, and many Bible scholars believe these are theophanies, manifestations of the pre-incarnate Christ. Other examples include the commander of the Lord's army in Joshua 5:13-15, and the fourth man in the fiery furnace in Daniel 3. It is also possible that these manifestations, including the man who speaks to Daniel here in Daniel 10, are angels. The biblical text does not tell us with certainty.

Princes of nations, princes of the spirit realm

When this man appeared before Daniel, only Daniel could see him. Yet Daniel's vision created such a spiritual and emotional shock-wave that all the people around him trembled, ran, and hid themselves, even though they had no idea what they were afraid of. So Daniel stood alone by the river as the vision continued—and it's clear that Daniel, too, was very much afraid. His face was pale and his hands and knees trembled uncontrollably. The man touched Daniel and said, "O Daniel, man greatly loved, understand the words that I speak to you, and stand upright, for now I have been sent to you. Fear not, Daniel, for from the first day that you set your heart to understand and humbled yourself before your God, your words have been heard, and I have come because of your words" (10:12).

Understand what the man is telling Daniel. He is saying that at the moment Daniel began to fast and pray (which, Daniel says, was three weeks earlier), God sent this man with the answer to his prayer. Why, then, did it take three weeks for this man to arrive with God's answer? The man goes on to explain: "The prince of the kingdom of Persia withstood me twenty-one days, but Michael, one of the chief princes, came to help me" (10:13). A battle took place between this supernatural man and the "prince of the kingdom of Persia." This battle lasted twenty-one days—three weeks—but then Michael, "one of the chief princes," came to the aid of this supernatural messenger.

This is the first mention in Scripture of the archangel Michael, who is mentioned again in Daniel 10:21 and 12:1, Jude 9, and Revelation 12:7. Clearly, Michael is a great warrior among the angels, and he is the prince of the people of Israel—a righteous prince, a servant of God, as opposed to the demon-princes, such as the prince of Persia. In 10:21, the man tells Daniel that Michael is "your prince" (meaning Israel's prince) and in 12:1 he calls Michael "the great prince who has charge of your people."

So nations appear to have spiritual entities or "princes" assigned to them. Some nations, such as Israel, have a righteous prince. Pagan nations like Persia have a demon-prince oppressing them. The "prince of the kingdom of Persia" is clearly a powerful demonic ruler, but Satan's demon-princes are no match for the angels of the Lord.

As the writer of the book of Hebrews observes, angels are "ministering spirits sent out to serve for the sake of those who are to inherit salvation" (Hebrews 1:14). We should not fear world events, even if the economy collapses, the social order crumbles, and the machines of war scream all around us. As the Lord has said to us through the psalmist:

> You will not fear the terror of the night,
>   nor the arrow that flies by day…
> For he will command his angels concerning you
>   to guard you in all your ways.
>   (Psalm 91:5,11)

We tend to think that God delays in answering our prayers. But this passage suggests that when we pray, God instantly begins to answer that request. The reason for the apparent delay is that God needs to work out all the circumstances in order for our prayers to be answered. In this case, God had to deal with the "prince of the kingdom of Persia," a demonic ruler who had dominion over the pagan, idol-worshipping nation of Persia. And remember, the *human* ruler of Persia was Cyrus. It may well be that the Lord was contending with the demonic prince of Persia for control of the will of Cyrus himself. In order for Daniel's prayer to be answered, God likely had to win a spiritual battle involving the heart and mind of the Persian emperor.

Even though God begins immediately to answer our prayers, from a human perspective it seems that the answers are often delayed. This is because we live in a fallen world—a world that is truly a spiritual battlefield between the forces of God and the forces of Satan. Demons oppose God's work, and many of these demonic spirits are assigned to the various nations of the earth. Once we understand that we are engaged in a struggle "against the rulers, against the authorities, against the cosmic powers over this present darkness, against the spiritual forces of evil in the heavenly places" (Ephesians 6:12), then many of the confusing events in this world—from our personal struggles to issues of terrorism and wars between nations—begin to pop into focus.

Later in Daniel 10, in verse 20, the supernatural messenger says to Daniel, "But now I will return to fight against the prince of Persia; and when I go out, behold, the prince of Greece will come." So in this glimpse of the spiritual battle that rages behind the walls of our visible world, we see two demonic enemies, the prince of Persia and the prince of Greece. As we look around the world today, as we see nations embroiled in conflict or persecuting Christians and Jews within their borders, it is not hard to imagine these nations being whipped up and controlled by demonic princes.

The next time you open the newspaper or turn on the TV news, remember Daniel's final vision. It reveals the existence of an invisible struggle between God's angels and the demonic forces that exercise authority over nations. These spiritual forces of evil are constantly striving against God and stirring up conflict, desperately trying to upset God's eternal plan. These evil forces cannot prevail. God's ultimate victory is assured. But in the meantime, the forces of evil have power to cause enormous destruction and inflict many casualties.

Israel in the crossfire

In chapter 11, the man continues his conversation with Daniel at the riverbank, telling him what is about to take place in world events. It is a lengthy and detailed description of numerous conflicts that would soon play out in regions to the north and south of Israel, with the Jewish nation caught in the middle.

"And as for me, in the first year of Darius the Mede, I stood up to confirm and strengthen him.

"And now I will show you the truth. Behold, three more kings shall arise in Persia, and a fourth shall be far richer than all of them. And when he has become strong through his riches, he shall stir up all against the kingdom of Greece. Then a mighty king shall arise, who shall rule with great dominion and do as he wills. And as soon as he has arisen, his kingdom shall be broken and divided toward the four winds of heaven, but not to his posterity, nor according to the authority with which he ruled, for his kingdom shall be plucked up and go to others besides these.

"Then the king of the south shall be strong, but one of his princes shall be stronger than he and shall rule, and his authority shall be a great authority. After some years they shall make an alliance, and the daughter of the king of the south shall come to the king of the north to make an agreement. But she shall not retain the strength of her arm, and he and his arm shall not endure, but she shall be given up, and her attendants, he who fathered her, and he who supported her in those times.

"And from a branch from her roots one shall arise in his place. He shall come against the army and enter the fortress of the king of the north, and he shall deal with them and shall prevail. He shall also carry off to Egypt their gods with their metal images and their precious vessels of silver and gold, and for some years he shall refrain from attacking the king of the north. Then the latter shall come into the realm of the king of the south but shall return to his own land.

"His sons shall wage war and assemble a multitude of great forces, which shall keep coming and overflow and pass through, and again shall carry the war as far as his fortress. Then the king of the south, moved with rage, shall come out and fight against the king of the north. And he shall raise a great multitude, but it shall be given into his hand. And when the multitude is taken away, his heart shall be exalted, and he shall cast down tens of thousands, but he shall not prevail. For the king of the north shall again raise a multitude, greater than the first. And after some years he shall come on with a great army and abundant supplies.

"In those times many shall rise against the king of the south, and the violent among your own people shall lift themselves up in order to fulfill the vision, but they shall fail. Then the king of the north shall come and throw up siegeworks and take a well-fortified city. And the forces of the south shall not stand, or even his best troops, for there shall be no strength to stand. But he who comes against him shall do as he wills, and none shall stand before him. And he shall stand in the glorious land, with destruction in his hand. He shall set his face to come with the strength of his whole kingdom, and he shall bring terms of an agreement and perform them. He shall give him the daughter of women to destroy the kingdom, but it shall not stand or be to his advantage. Afterward he shall turn his face to the coastlands and shall capture many of them, but a commander shall put an end to his insolence. Indeed, he shall turn his insolence back upon him. Then he shall turn his face back toward the fortresses of his own land, but he shall stumble and fall, and shall not be found.

"Then shall arise in his place one who shall send an exactor of tribute for the glory of the kingdom. But within a few days he shall be broken, neither in anger nor in battle. In his place shall arise a contemptible person to whom royal majesty has not been given. He shall come in without warning and obtain the kingdom by flatteries. Armies shall be utterly swept away before him and broken, even the prince of the covenant. And from the time that an alliance is made with him he shall act deceitfully, and he shall become strong with a small people. Without warning he shall come into the richest parts of the province, and he shall do what neither his fathers nor his fathers' fathers have done, scattering among them plunder, spoil, and goods. He shall devise plans against strongholds, but only for a time. And he shall stir up his power and his heart against the king of the south with a great army. And the king of the south shall wage war with an exceedingly great and mighty army, but he shall not stand, for plots shall be devised against him. Even those who eat his food shall break him. His army shall be swept away, and many shall fall down slain. And as for the two kings, their hearts shall be bent on doing evil. They shall speak lies at the same table, but to no avail, for the end is yet to be at the time appointed. And he shall return to his land with great wealth, but his heart shall be set against the holy covenant. And he shall work his will and return to his own land.

"At the time appointed he shall return and come into the south, but it shall not be this time as it was before. For ships of Kittim shall come against him, and he shall be afraid and withdraw, and shall turn back and be enraged and take action against the holy covenant. He shall turn back and pay attention to those who forsake the holy covenant. Forces from him shall appear and profane the temple and fortress, and shall take away the regular burnt offering. And they shall set up the abomination that makes desolate. He shall seduce with flattery those who violate the covenant, but the people who know their God shall stand firm and take action. And the wise among the people shall make many understand, though for some days they shall stumble by sword and flame, by captivity and plunder. When they stumble, they shall receive a little help. And many shall join themselves to them with flattery, and some of the wise shall stumble, so that they may be refined, purified, and made white, until the time of the end, for it still awaits the appointed time.

"And the king shall do as he wills. He shall exalt himself and magnify himself above every god, and shall speak astonishing things against the God of gods. He shall prosper till the indignation is accomplished; for what is decreed shall be done. He shall pay no attention to the gods of his fathers, or to the one beloved by women. He shall not pay attention to any other god, for he shall magnify himself above all. He shall honor the god of fortresses instead of these. A god whom his fathers did not know he shall honor with gold and silver, with precious stones and costly gifts. He shall deal with the strongest fortresses with the help of a foreign god. Those who acknowledge him he shall load with honor. He shall make them rulers over many and shall divide the land for a price.

"At the time of the end, the king of the south shall attack him, but the king of the north shall rush upon him like a whirlwind, with chariots and horsemen, and with many ships. And he shall come into countries and shall overflow and pass through. He shall come into the glorious land. And tens of thousands shall fall, but these shall be delivered out of his hand: Edom and Moab and the main part of the Ammonites. He shall stretch out his hand against the countries, and the land of Egypt shall not escape. He shall become ruler of the treasures of gold and of silver, and all the precious things of Egypt, and the Libyans and the Cushites shall follow in his train. But news from the east and the north shall alarm him, and he shall go out with great fury to destroy and devote many to destruction. And he shall pitch his palatial tents between the sea and the glorious holy mountain. Yet he shall come to his end, with none to help him" (11:1-45).

Daniel 11 relates a prophecy that has largely been fulfilled. It foretells an epic struggle between Seleucid Syria ("the king of the north") and Ptolemaic Egypt ("the king of the south")—a struggle that was played out after the death of Daniel. The events, which took place over a period of at least two centuries, were foretold in surprising detail. The phrase "the daughter of the king of the south" (11:6) is widely believed to be a reference to Berenice, the daughter of Ptolemy II Philadelphus, though some think it may refer to Cleopatra.

Egypt and Syria battled often, almost continually, for more than a century—and Israel, because of its geographic location, was caught in the crossfire. As the armies surged northward and southward, the plains of Israel and Judah became battlefields. The city of Jerusalem was besieged and beset a number of times. This account depicts Israel as an unwilling participant in the wars between neighboring kingdoms.

Be strong and of good courage

One of the most striking themes that winds its way through Daniel 10 and 11 is the theme of fear. When the messenger first appears to Daniel at the riverbank, the people around Daniel are struck by fear. They flee in terror, even though they cannot see the man and don't even know what they are afraid of. And as for Daniel, his knees are knocking like castanets and his hands are quaking like aspen leaves.

In 10:12, the man has to reassure him, "Fear not, Daniel, for from the first day that you set your heart to understand and humbled yourself before your God, your words have been heard, and I have come because of your words." Again in 10:18, a fearful Daniel receives words of encouragement and reassurance from the mysterious messenger: "O man greatly loved, fear not, peace be with you; be strong and of good courage." The visions Daniel relates in chapters 10 and 11 filled him with deep distress, but the messenger calms him with a message of peace.

At this time in his life, Daniel is in his eighties. He has been through many harrowing experiences, and he has faced them all with faith and courage. His nation was conquered by Babylonian invaders, his city was destroyed, his people were slaughtered or led in chains into exile in Babylon. Enemies plotted against his life. His friends were thrown into a fiery furnace. He himself spent a night in a den of lions. He has looked death and torture in the face many times, and each time he has been delivered—sometimes miraculously—by his Lord.

But here, in these verses, we see Daniel stricken and paralyzed with fear. Where is his faith? Where is his spiritual maturity? Where is his trust in God?

It's all still there. Daniel is still a man of faith, still a man of deep, godly character. But he is human. I think we make a mistake by placing Daniel on too high a pedestal. We make a mistake by supposing that, during his march into exile or during his bold stand before Nebuchadnezzar or during his descent into the lions' den, he felt no fear.

Daniel was no plaster saint. He was a flesh-and-blood man. He had the same fight-or-flight impulses built into his brain, the same sense of self-preservation, the same adrenaline surging in his blood-stream as you or I would have in those circumstances. He trembled—yet he trusted. His face went pale—yet he kept his eyes on the Lord.

Are you ever afraid? Of course you are! So am I. God's message to you is the same as his message to Daniel: "O Christian greatly loved, fear not, peace be with you; be strong and of good courage." As Jesus himself told us:

> "Therefore do not be anxious, saying, 'What shall we eat?' or 'What shall we drink?' or 'What shall we wear?' For the Gentiles seek after all these things, and your heavenly Father knows that you need them all. But seek first the kingdom of God and his righteousness, and all these things will be added to you.
>
> "Therefore do not be anxious about tomorrow, for tomorrow will be anxious for itself. Sufficient for the day is its own trouble" (Matthew 6:31-34).

So don't let events in the news shake your confidence in the Lord. Don't let a financial loss or an automobile accident or the death of a loved one or a cancer diagnosis or any other worry or catastrophe shake your confidence in the Lord. Don't let the prophecies of the end times make you afraid. O friend in Christ, loved by God, cherished as his child—fear not, peace be with you.

Be strong and of good courage, because God will be with us throughout the days ahead.

16

The Time of the End

Daniel 12

Once, after I had spoken to a group about prayer, one person came to me afterward and said, "Pastor, God reminds me of my mother."

"Your mother?" I said. "What do you mean?"

"My mother used to tell me to do things, and when I asked her *why*, she'd say, 'Because I said so.' When I asked her *when* such-and-such would happen, she'd say, 'When the time is right.' When I asked her *how* she was going to do this or that, she'd say, 'I'm going to do it the right way.' When I asked her *what* kind of surprise she had planned for me, she'd say, 'You'll find out—and you'll like it.' God's answers sound just like my mother's."

It's true that, in many ways, God does ask us to trust him completely. When we ask him why or when or how or what, his answer to us is simply, "I am the Lord. You're not. Trust me."

If you have a godly, biblical perspective, then you know that is actually a very good answer. He *is* the Lord. He *is* trustworthy and unchanging. He *is* all-knowing, all-powerful, and all-caring. If anyone can be trusted, it is God Most High, Creator of heaven and earth. If you are looking for something to cling to, cling to God's promises. If his answer to your prayer is, "Wait and see," then whatever he is preparing will be more than worth the wait.

Times of sorrow and suffering

The twelfth and final chapter of Daniel deals with the final chapter of history, the time of the end. It is a future time of intense trouble for the nation of Israel. The Jewish people have known times of sorrow and suffering throughout their history. Satan has repeatedly marked the Jews for extinction precisely because they are God's chosen people. From the fall of Jerusalem and the exile to Babylon to the horrors and blasphemies of Antiochus Epiphanes to the destruction of Jerusalem by the Romans in AD 70 to the centuries of pogroms and persecutions in Europe to the Nazi Holocaust to the Middle East wars, the Jews have suffered grievously.

But Daniel 12 describes a future time of trouble that will be far worse than any other calamity in Israel's history.

> "At that time shall arise Michael, the great prince who has charge of your people. And there shall be a time of trouble, such as never has been since there was a nation till that time. But at that time your people shall be delivered, everyone whose name shall be found written in the book. And many of those who sleep in the dust of the earth shall awake, some to everlasting life, and some to shame and everlasting contempt. And those who are wise shall shine like the brightness of the sky above; and those who turn many to righteousness, like the stars forever and ever. But you, Daniel, shut up the words and seal the book, until the time of the end. Many shall run to and fro, and knowledge shall increase" (12:1-4).

The archangel Michael is a warrior angel and the guardian angel of the Jewish people. He is, in fact, the prince of Israel. In the last days, Michael shall stand up, "the great prince who has charge of your people," and then "there shall be a time of trouble, such as never has been since there was a nation till that time" (12:1). As we have already seen, the archangel Michael is associated in Scripture with spiritual warfare (see Daniel 10:13 and 21, Jude 9, and Revelation 12:7). And Michael's opponent in the battle will be Satan himself.

People often think of Satan as the opposite of God, but that is not true. God has no opposite. The true opposite of Satan is Michael the high-ranking angel (which is what *archangel* means). The time that is spoken of in this prophecy is a period of global calamity and persecution known as the Great Tribulation. This period, also known as "the time of Jacob's trouble," is also predicted by the prophet Jeremiah:

> "Alas! That day is so great
>   there is none like it;
> it is a time of distress for Jacob;
>   yet he shall be saved out of it."
>   (Jeremiah 30:7)

Jesus refers to the Great Tribulation in his Olivet Discourse, a private teaching session he had with some of his disciples on the Mount of Olives, in which he taught about the last days.

> "So when you see the abomination of desolation spoken of by the prophet Daniel, standing in the holy place (let the reader understand), then let those who are in Judea flee to the mountains. Let the one who is on the housetop not go down to take what is in his house, and let the one who is in the field not turn back to take his cloak. And alas for women who are pregnant and for those who are nursing infants in those days! Pray that your flight may not be in winter or on a Sabbath. For

then there will be great tribulation, such as has not been from the beginning of the world until now, no, and never will be. And if those days had not been cut short, no human being would be saved. But for the sake of the elect those days will be cut short" (Matthew 24:15-22).

And Revelation 12:13-17 also describes a Great Tribulation, a time when God's people will once again—and for the final time in history—be targeted for destruction by Satan and the Antichrist. But God and the archangel Michael will prevail over Satan. In spite of the horrors suffered by the Jewish people during the Great Tribulation, they will be delivered. God will keep the promise he made to Abraham:

"And I will establish my covenant between me and you and your offspring after you throughout their generations for an everlasting covenant, to be God to you and to your offspring after you" (Genesis 17:7).

This promise is now fulfilled in Jesus who is the descendant of Abraham. God always keeps his promises. That is why the early church was made up primarily of Jewish believers, and in the end many Jews will put their whole trust in their Messiah.

"Shut up the words and seal the book"

As the man tells Daniel in this prophecy, "But at that time your people shall be delivered, everyone whose name shall be found written in the book" (12:1). Clearly, not every person of Jewish heritage is destined for salvation. But those whose names are found written in the book will be saved, and the people of Israel will receive their Messiah. It will be the fulfillment of God's promise through the prophet Jeremiah:

"For this is the covenant that I will make with the house of Israel after those days, declares the LORD: I will put my law within them, and I will write it on their hearts. And I will be their God, and they shall be my people" (Jeremiah 31:33).

In this prophecy, we also see a clear teaching about the resurrection of the dead: "And many of those who sleep in the dust of the earth shall awake, some to everlasting life, and some to shame and everlasting contempt" (12:2). Here, the Scriptures speak clearly of two different destinies—everlasting life for the saved and everlasting shame and contempt for the unsaved. There are those, including some in the church, who have abandoned this doctrine, and who teach there is no hell, no everlasting damnation, for the unbeliever. Don't be fooled. Compare this teaching in Daniel with the parallel passages in the New Testament, including John 5:28-29 and Revelation 20:4-6,11-15.

Next, Daniel is instructed to "shut up the words, and seal the book until the time of the end" (12:4). To shut up the words suggests that these words will be safeguarded until a time when they are truly needed. To seal the book suggests that its message must be officially authenticated—as when a king would seal a document by pressing his signet into sealing wax. These instructions indicate that, while the prophecy was valid in Daniel's day and remains valid in our day, its message will be even more intensely valuable and relevant at "the time of the end."

The prophecy also speaks of a time when "many shall run to and fro, and knowledge shall increase"—phrases to remember the next time you are seated on a jetliner, speeding to a distant city while surfing the Internet on your iPad or smartphone. These words, describing what "the time of the end" will be like, suggest that the times described in this prophecy might not be far away.

"A time, times, and half a time"

Next, Daniel looks and sees not one but two men standing at the river's edge, one on either side of the river. One of them asks the man clothed in linen, the man Daniel saw in his terrifying vision back in Daniel 10:5, "How long shall it be till the end of these wonders?" This man clothed in linen then delivers a message to Daniel that is strangely specific regarding certain events at the time of the end:

> Then I, Daniel, looked, and behold, two others stood, one on this bank of the stream and one on that bank of the stream. And someone said to the man clothed in linen, who was above the waters of the stream, "How long shall it be till the end of these wonders?" And I heard the man clothed in linen, who was above the waters of the stream; he raised his right hand and his left hand toward heaven and swore by him who lives forever that it would be for a time, times, and half a time, and that when the shattering of the power of the holy people comes to an end all these things would be finished. I heard, but I did not understand. Then I said, "O my lord, what shall be the outcome of these things?" He said, "Go your way, Daniel, for the words are shut up and sealed until the time of the end. Many shall purify themselves and make themselves white and be refined, but the wicked shall act wickedly. And none of the wicked shall understand, but those who are wise shall understand. And from the time that the regular burnt offering is taken away and the abomination that makes desolate is set up, there shall be 1,290 days. Blessed is he who waits and arrives at the 1,335 days. But go your way till the end. And you shall rest and shall stand in your allotted place at the end of the days" (12:5-13).

It may well be that this scene depicts an angel asking the preincarnate Lord about the schedule for the time of the end. Or it may be that all three of these figures are angels. In any case, one of them asks when these prophesied events will end, and the one who was above the river replies with a solemn oath, "a time, times, and half a time" (12:7).

This odd phrase is generally thought to mean three and a half years (a year, plus two years, plus half a year). It is used here in parallel with "1,290 days" (12:11). This same formulation for three and a half years appears elsewhere in Scripture, in Daniel 7:25 and Revelation 12:14. Now, if you are good at math, you may have already noticed that if you add up "a time, times, and half a time"—one 360-day year, two more 360-day years, plus a 180-day half-year—you get a total of 1260 days, not 1290 days. For some reason that we probably can't understand today, this prophecy adds a 30-day "leap month" to bring the total of days to 1290. The reason for this "leap month" is unclear now, but will probably be clear at the time this prophecy comes to pass.

The prophecy of Daniel 12 is underscored by a solemn oath and by what appears to be a miracle that all Christians should recognize: the linen-clothed man who speaks to Daniel walks on water—or as Daniel puts it, he "was above the waters of the stream." The man raises his right hand, points his left hand toward heaven, and makes an oath by "him who lives forever" that this three and a half year period will take place—then these things will be finished.

This three and a half year period seems to correspond with the time that the holy city of Jerusalem will be overrun by Gentiles (Revelation 11:2), the time when two prophetic witnesses will preach the gospel in Israel (Revelation 11:3), the time of Israel's tribulation (Revelation 12:6,14), and the time of Antichrist's blasphemous and murderous rule (Revelation 13:5). This, then, is the last half of the Great Tribulation, also known as "Daniel's seventieth week."

Don't fear the future

Many books have been written and sermons preached about those times. Many arguments and debates have been launched by the prophetic passages of God's Word, including this passage. But I am inclined to second the words of Daniel himself, who upon hearing this prophecy, said, "I heard, but I did not understand" (12:8).

I don't think you and I were meant to fully understand these matters—not until these events come to fruition. If Daniel was not meant to understand them, then how can we claim to know more than he did? When Daniel said, "O my lord, what shall be the outcome of these things?" (12:8), the man clothed in linen replied, "Go your way, Daniel, for the words are shut up and sealed until the time of the end" (12:9). I think that command applies to you and me as well.

What then are we supposed to do with this prophecy? We should make sure that we are faithful, that our hearts are right with God, and that our names are found written in the book. As the man clothed in linen told Daniel, "Many shall purify themselves and make themselves white and be refined, but the wicked shall act wickedly. And none of the wicked shall understand, but those who are wise shall understand" (12:10).

Are we wise? Do we understand what God wants from us? Have we purified ourselves from sin? Have we refined ourselves through our obedience to God?

I believe God wants from us the same things he wanted from Daniel: trust, faithfulness, obedience, love, and lifelong devotion. Daniel gave all these things to the Lord throughout his life. And God entrusted to Daniel a vision of the time of the end. Daniel faithfully recorded that vision just as it was given to him, even though he could not fully understand what it meant.

One day, all that is murky now will be as clear and sharply etched as crystal. One day, these future events will shift into the past. What is now foretold will be hindsight. All mysteries will be revealed, the wisdom of God will be exalted, and the Lord Most High will be glorified.

Are you ready for that day to come? Is your name written in the book? When the dead are raised, will you be raised to everlasting life—or to shame and everlasting contempt? Do you fear the time of the end prophesied in Daniel 12? Or do you welcome the future, even with all its terrors and uncertainties, knowing that God is in control?

God did not give these visions to Daniel just to give him one more thing to worry about. He gave these visions to Daniel so that he would write them down and pass them on to future generations. He gave them to Daniel so that they would be shut up and sealed for a time when they would be needed. God trusted Daniel to "write it right" for those who would follow.

But God didn't intend for Daniel to become obsessed with this prophecy in an unhealthy way. He wanted Daniel to live out his life, serving God and serving others, until the end of his days. That's why the messenger said to Daniel, "But go your way till the end. And you shall rest and shall stand in your allotted place at the end of the days" (12:13).

Daniel's inheritance would be waiting for him at the time of the end. So God's word to Daniel was to simply live out his life to the best of his ability, trusting and obeying, and leaving all the outcomes to God. And that is God's word to you and me as well. Let's not be anxious. Let's not be fearful. Let's not be obsessed with trying to figure out the unknowable future. Let's leave tomorrow in God's hands.

Those whose names are written in the book have no reason to fear the time of the end. As Jesus said to a man who came and questioned him late one night, "For God so loved the world, that he gave his only Son, that whoever believes in him should not perish but have eternal life" (John 3:16).

Believe Jesus. And believe *in* Jesus.

And *live*.

Notes

1. Tony Harris and Kyra Phillips, "Live From," March 15, 2005, CNN.com, http://transcripts.cnn.com/TRANSCRIPTS/0503/15/lol.04.html.

2. Elbert Hubbard, *Selected Writings of Elbert Hubbard: Philistia* (New York: William H. Wise, 1922), 20-21.

3. Ernest C. Cowper, letter to Elbert Hubbard II (son of Elbert and Alice Hubbard), March 12, 1916, "Elbert Hubbard," RoycroftCampusCorporation.com, www.roycroftcampuscorporation.com/hubbard.html.

4. John Paton with James Paton, *The Story of John G. Paton, or Thirty Years Among South Sea Cannibals*, 1891, Gutenberg.org, www.gutenberg.org/files/28025/28025-h/28025-h.htm.

5. Jay Dennis with Marilyn Jeffcoat, *The Jabez Prayer Experiment: Discovering a Prayer That Could Change Your World* (Grand Rapids, MI: Zondervan, 2001), 92.

6. High Flight Foundation, "About Us," HighFlightFoundation.org, 2012, www.highflightfoundation.org/about_us.

7. Sir Isaac Newton, *Observations upon the Prophecies of Daniel and the Apocalypse of St. John* (London: J. Darby and T. Browne, 1733), www.gutenberg.org/files/16878/16878-h/16878-h.htm.

8. Ibid.

9. James H. Jeans, *The Growth of Physical Science* (Cambridge, England: The University Press, 1947), 7.

10. Bob Becking, Alex Cannegieter, Wilfred van de Poll, and Anne-Mareike Wetter, *From Babylon to Eternity: The Exile Remembered and Constructed in Text and Tradition* (Sheffield, England: Equinox, 2010), 25.

About Michael Youssef

Michael Youssef was born in Egypt and came to America in his late twenties in 1977. He received a master's degree in theology from Fuller Theological Seminary in California and a PhD in social anthropology from Emory University. Michael served for nearly ten years with the Haggai Institute, traveling around the world teaching courses in evangelism and church leadership to church leaders. He rose to the position of managing director at the age of thirty-one. The family settled in Atlanta, and in 1984, Michael became a United States citizen, fulfilling a dream he had held for many years.

Dr. Youssef founded The Church of the Apostles in 1987 with fewer than forty adults with the mission to "equip the saints and seek the lost." The church has since grown to a congregation of over three thousand. This church on a hill was the launching pad for Leading the Way, an international ministry whose radio and television programs are heard by millions at home and abroad.

For more on Michael Youssef, The Church of the Apostles, and Leading the Way, visit apostles.org and www.leadingtheway.org.

Leading the Way Through the Bible Commentary Series

About the Series: The Leading the Way Through the Bible commentary series will not only increase readers' Bible knowledge, but it will motivate readers to apply God's Word to the problems of our hurting world and to a deeper and more obedient walk with Jesus Christ. The writing is lively, informal, and packed with stories that illustrate the truth of God's Word. The Leading the Way series is a call to action—and a call to the exciting adventure of living for Christ.

LEADING THE WAY THROUGH EPHESIANS

Throughout the book of Ephesians, Paul refers to "the riches of God's grace," "our riches in Christ," and "the riches of His glory" as he reminds believers of the spiritual treasures they already possess in Christ. *Leading the Way through Ephesians* applies these great truths in such practical areas of the Christian life as

- enduring trials, suffering, and persecution
- maintaining the unity of the church through Christian love
- living out the gospel in our marriages and family relationships
- praying with power
- maintaining our armor against the attacks of Satan

Through vibrant illustrations, a brisk conversational style, and sound teaching that applies God's truth to the realities of the twenty-first century, *Leading the Way through Ephesians* will show readers the way to a stronger, more active, more dynamic faith.

> ### Coming in March 2013:
> *Leading the Way Through Joshua*
> *Leading the Way Through Galatians*